44 W

Lyle E. Schaller

Illustrated by Edward Lee Tucker

44 Ways to Revitalize the Women's Organization

Abingdon Press
Nashville

44 WAYS TO REVITALIZE THE WOMEN'S ORGANIZATION

Copyright ©1990 by Abingdon Press

This book is printed on acid-free paper.

Library of Congress Cataloging-in-Publication Data

Schaller, Lyle E.
44 ways to revitalize the women's organization / Lyle E. Schaller; illustrated by Edward Lee Tucker.
p. cm.
Includes bibliographical references.
ISBN 0-687-13288-6 (alk. paper)
1. Women in church work—Societies. etc. I. Title. II. Title: Forty-four ways to revitalize the women's organization.
BV4420.S33   1990
267'.4—dc20   89-36757
                                                              CIP

94 95 96 97 98 99 00 01 02 03 04 — 10 9 8 7 6 5 4

MANUFACTURED IN THE UNITED STATES OF AMERICA

TO

Agnes O'Bryan Peterson
Elizabeth Peterson Del Nero
Marianna Allen Peterson
Grace Brandt Schaller

Sandra G. Clopine
Maggie Day
Betty A. Duda
Bonnie L. Frazier
Nina G. Gunter
Doris R. Johnson
Jackie Oeach
Diana J. Paulsen
Sarah Regier
Carolyn Weatherford

Connie Beth Chilton
Mary Ellen Ingram
Gerry Kramer
Virginia Osborne
Janice Perkins
Phyllis Reedy
Jane Vann
Eleanor Wang

Contents

3 1933 05650 3422

Introduction

The reader of any book has a right to ask why it was written and to inquire about the assumptions and biases of the author.

The first of the ten basic assumptions on which this book rests is that in several denominations, and in thousands of congregations, the women's fellowships have been an exceptionally valuable component of the organizational life. In many churches they have offered the most effective educational ministry provided by that congregation. Until recently

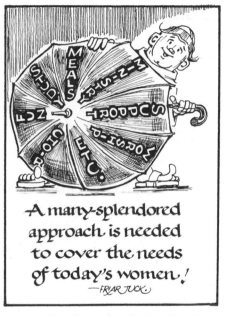

A many-splendored approach is needed to cover the needs of today's women!
—FRIAR TUCK

the women's organizations and the Sunday schools led all of American Protestantism in encouraging adults to engage themselves in serious study of the Holy Scripture. The women's organizations also have been the number-one advocate for missions. Their leaders have mastered a remarkably high level of competence in organizational skills. The women's organizations have been the most sensitive of all religious groups on social action concerns and on issue-centered ministries. The thousands of local fellowships have provided attractive entry points for impressive numbers of newcomers to that congregation. They have been an effective channel for assimilating newcomers into the life and ministry of that congregation. Frequently, they have provided the best system for identifying, enlisting, training, and placing a new generation of leaders of any organization in American Protestantism. For several decades in at least a dozen denominational families the women's organization has been the financial backbone of that denomination's missionary program. Women's organizations have an enviable record in challenging and enlisting young people for full-time Christian service in the mission field. If God published a record of prayers directed to Him, the record undoubtedly would reveal that a disproportionately large number have been offered by women gathered in missionary groups. If, as many believe, the world missionary effort of American Protestantism has been sustained by prayers for the past eighteen decades, a disproportionately large segment of those prayers have been inspired by the women's organizations.

The various women's organizations in several denominations have displayed a unique sensitivity to the changes brought by the passage of time and have compiled an outstanding record of creativity in identifying and witnessing to new needs. The circles and groups in local fellowships have provided redemptive mutual support groups for tens of thousands of women who find themselves living alone in their golden years. Finally, the women's organizations, both nationally and congregationally, have challenged the men to be more faithful in their witness, to be more obedient to the call of the Lord, and to be more sensitive to the needs of others.

That is the number-one assumption on which this book rests. The second assumption is it would be a shame to write off that resource on the basis that a more egalitarian society has made the women's organization an anachronism.

The third assumption is that the missionary movement is still alive and well and that can be a powerful central organizing principle for building a women's organization. A big policy question, which is discussed in the first chapter and repeatedly in subsequent chapters, is whether or not missions should be the only focal point of a women's fellowship.

A fourth assumption is that the vast majority of Protestant

congregations on the North American continent do not offer a comprehensive program that can meet all the religious needs of all the people. (That is the greatest understatement of reality in this book!) Thus for readers who want to broaden the umbrella that describes the purpose of the women's organization, a huge range of possibilities exist. One means of revitalizing the women's organization could be to expand that statement of purpose, redefine the role, and enlarge the program to respond to the religious needs of people that are not being met by the rest of the ministries of that congregation. The other half of that argument is if those needs have been identified, if no other organization or group in that congregation is willing to respond, perhaps the women's fellowship should take the initiative in filling that vacuum.

A fifth assumption is that a large number of women still believe in the need for an all-female organization in the local church. Many of them share the conviction that this glorious record has not been made obsolete by the changing times. Many of these women agree the old ways no longer are working and are open to new approaches to ministry through the women's organization. They are convinced new initiatives are needed to reach a new generation of women. They share the conviction of the authors that God still has a place in His plan for the women's organization and that the call to be faithful and obedient is stronger than the call to do yesterday over again. These women understand why some men are more comfortable in an all-male group and often avoid gatherings that include women. Likewise some women find it easier to enter the life and ministry of a congregation through an all-female organization.

They also understand that, contrary to conventional wisdom, the influx of women into the paid labor force has not destroyed the place for a women's fellowship. It is true that the proportion of women working at a full-time job on a year-around basis rose from 40.1 percent in 1966 to 49.5 percent in 1986, but it also is true the number of women in the 35-69 age bracket who are *not* employed outside the home was slightly less than 20 million in 1988, the same number as in 1950 and 1970. (Earl F. Mellor and William Parks II, "A

Year's Work: labor force activity from a different perspective," *Monthly Labor Review,* September 1988, pp. 13-18.) The number of women aged 45 and over who are *not* in the labor force rose from 18.4 million in 1960 to 27.3 million in 1988. More significant is the research that reveals no difference in church attendance patterns between women employed full-time and those who are not in the paid labor force or those working part-time.

These women who affirm the value of an all-female organization also recognize and are aware that the three big "winners" in determining how women spend their discretionary time are (1) highly structured women's Bible study groups with trained leadership that meet during the week, (2) personal health, including jogging, swimming, and aerobic dance classes, and (3) marital concerns, including the growing number of Mother's Clubs, marriage enrichment and marriage encounter retreats, mutual support groups for the recently divorced and single parent fellowships. This is the audience to which this book is directed.

A sixth assumption, which should not have to be stated, is that it is good for people to be part of a worshiping community. It is an essential part of Christian life to join with others in worshiping God, in praising Him, and in hearing His word proclaimed. For some women the most attractive entry point into God's church will be through the women's fellowship in the company of other women. This is especially true of that growing number of women who live alone and may be repelled by the image, "This is a family church." A circle in the women's fellowship can be an attractive entry point for these women.

Likewise it is assumed that evangelism cannot be delegated to the pastor or to one committee, but must be a part of every facet of the life and ministry of every Christian community. The women's fellowship is not an exception to that generalization. Therefore it is assumed throughout this book that a women's fellowship exists not only to serve the women of that congregation, but also to reach out beyond the membership to others.

An eighth assumption is it is not only legitimate, but it is

also a central teaching of the faith that Christians be responsive to all the needs of all God's children. Thus it is appropriate for a women's fellowship to feed the hungry, to visit those
in jail, to clothe the naked, and to comfort the lonely. These
are opportunities to respond to the call to be a faithful servant
as well as to the call to be a witness to Christ's redeeming love.
Critics may ask what is the difference between a social welfare
program offered by the church and that administered by a
secular or government agency. The answer to that question
always begins with the question of why that program has been
initiated. For the Christian the documentation is in the two
great commandments of Jesus.

A ninth and overlapping assumption is that by its very
nature a women's fellowship should not allow itself to become
a private club, but must include outreach to others as its
central purpose. The debate can be over the form and extent
of that outreach beyond the membership, but not over
outreach as the central reason for being.

The Salvation Army has articulated that quality with the
declaration that members are asked to extend a "hand to
man" and to give their "heart to God."

Finally, and some readers may find this to be highly
presumptuous, it is assumed here that it is acceptable for two
aging males to collaborate on a book about the women's
organization in the church. Part of the rationale is the
collaboration is broader than it appears. Back in the mid and
late 1980s we offered around the country a series of overnight workshops on the subject, "What's Ahead for the
Women's Organization?" In all but one of these the applica-
tions were at least double the number we could accommodate. This suggested that despite the male leadership a need
existed. The fact that scores of women came, often at
considerable sacrifice in terms of costs and inconvenience,
provided a powerful witness to the widespread concern about
the future of the women's organization. Equally important,
many of the women who came voiced crucial insights, raised
important questions, offered brilliant suggestions, shared
meaningful experiences, and suggested corrective changes.

Many of those participants will recognize their distinctive contributions in the text.

In addition, during the past three decades the senior author has been involved in hundreds of parish consultations that included interviews with leaders and members from the women's fellowship of that church as well as with women who chose not to be a part of it and often were remarkably candid in explaining their reasons.

As a part of that effort to broaden the data base, a dozen different leaders from the national women's organization of various denominations also have been exceptionally generous, courteous, and helpful in responding to my inquiries by mail—and in several cases this involved extensive correspondence.

To all these committed women we owe a huge debt of gratitude for their comments, cooperation, corrections, courtesy, creativity, criticisms, ideas, insights, patience, questions, recommendations, reflections, stories, suggestions, and thoughtfulness.

Dozens of readers have urged that every book needs a road map at the beginning to help the traveler understand the context for this shared journey and to be able to anticipate what lies ahead in the next chapter.

The first chapter is addressed to the policy makers in congregations, regional judicatories, and the national boards and staff of the women's organization. This chapter identifies and discusses twenty basic policy questions including the tradeoffs that must be faced. These twenty policy questions provide a context for the discussion that follows and especially for the suggestions in chapter 5. What are the acceptable tradeoffs?

Some readers may want to skip that first chapter (except for studying Friar Tuck's cartoons) and begin with the two scenarios described in the second chapter. At least a few readers will find this to be familiar territory. The theme is to contrast unintentional counterproductive behavior with a more intentional effort to lead a women's organization into a new era.

Those who are anxious to review the forty-four ways

promised in the title will have to wait for chapter 3 for the first
of the forty-four. The closest to a guaranteed way to revitalize
any long-established organization is new, dynamic, future-
oriented, creative, and aggressive leadership. This third
chapter is the story of that kind of leadership.

A big source of frustration for many leaders in the women's
organization is what to do about those monthly general
meetings. One response is to see them as the second best
approach to revitalizing the women's fellowship. Suggestions
on how that can be done constitute the fourth chapter under
the leadership of the composite figure of Susan Brown.

A long fifth chapter suggests forty-two other approaches to
revitalizing the women's organization. By this time the purists
will note that the generic term "women" is used, except when
the word "woman" is used as part of the proper name of a
particular organization. This has not been done as part of an
effort to lobby for the use of the plural rather than the
singular, but simply for purposes of internal consistency. No
offense is intended toward those who insist on using the
singular.

A word also needs to be said about use of the cartoons
scattered throughout this volume. The second paragraph
under the copyright notice states the conditions that will
allow you to utilize these cartoons as you turn to Friar Tuck
for help in revitalizing the women's organization in your
church.

Those who recall Paul Simon's clever song, "Fifty Ways to
Leave Your Lover," may ask why this book offers only
forty-four. One answer is that we are not as creative as Mr.
Simon. A second is that this book does include all forty-four
ways. It does not stop after brief bits of advice to Jack, Stan,
Roy, Gus, and Lee. A third response is that both Simon's song
and this book only introduce an idea; neither suggests the
number is a ceiling. In each the goal is to help one recognize
that scores of alternatives are open.

So, create a women's chorale, Sal. Find some women
interested in liturgical dance, Nance. Adopt a seminary
library, Mary. Enlist folks to go on a trip, Kip. Open the door

wider and invite a man, Jan. Organize a circle around learning a new skill, Jill. Challenge the women to a walka-thon, Allison.

In other words, we hope you can revitalize the women's organization in your church and have fun doing so, Jo.

CHAPTER ONE

Decisions and Tradeoffs

It is shortsighted to develop a long-term strategy for the women's organization in any congregation—or denomination—without first examining several policy questions. The decisions made in response to these questions will influence the direction, the role, the attractiveness, the constituency, the program, and the future of the women's organization.

Women or Missions?

The first, the most divisive, and the most influential of these policy questions can be introduced by a simple question, Will this be primarily a women's organization or *primarily* a missionary organization?

Perhaps the best beginning point for discussing that question is to look back in history. During the middle of the nineteenth century the Lutheran mission society of Sweden sent scores of pastors to the United States. When they came together to create the Augustana Synod in 1860 (that became known later as The Evangelical Lutheran Augustana Church of North America), they conceived of the church as a great mission society. It was expected that leaders from parishes would come together regularly at district meetings to promote and fund missions—including the support of mission societies in Europe.

Thirty-two years later, when the Augustana Synod met for its annual convention in Lindsborg, Kansas, Emmy Ewald, the daughter of a pastor and the wife of a pastor, brought a group of women together. Three days later the all-male delegation to the Synod Convention received Mrs. Ewald's

LADIES, WHEN YOU'RE DONE WITH THE DISHES DON'T FORGET TO TURN IN YOUR MONEY!

KITCHEN IN   KITCHEN OUT

For years, fund-raising and men have dominated the direction of most women's groups!

—FRIAR TUCK

proposal for the organization of a Women's Missionary Society. After a long debate the men approved Emmy Ewald's proposal. For the next quarter century the women raised more money for missions each year than did the Synod.

When 11,000 women came together on May 13-14, 1988, in Richmond, Virginia, to celebrate the centennial of the Woman's Missionary Union, they recalled how the WMU had rescued Southern Baptists' missionary efforts from financial disaster during the Great Depression of the 1930s. They also watched a drama group reenact the great debate of a century earlier as the men, who controlled the Southern Baptist Convention, opposed creation of a national women's organization. Many of the men feared this would encourage women to leave the home and seek to enter the pulpit. Eventually, the men concurred with the stipulation the women "will send us the money." They did! During the first century of its existence the WMU helped raise over $1 billion for missions!

On an earlier occasion, Miss Carolyn Weatherford, the recently retired executive director of the WMU, made an eloquent speech in which she expressed her basic philosophy and also defined the role of this auxiliary: "Anyone who knows the WMU knows that we are not a women's organization that happens to support missions. We are a missions organization that happens to be composed of women. Missions is our purpose, our lifeblood, our heritage, and our future."

In several other denominations the women's organization

traces its history back to an emphasis on missions. In 1800, for example, Mary Webb and other Baptist and Congregationalist women in Massachusetts came together to form the Boston Female Society for Missionary Purposes. In 1871 the Woman's American Baptist Foreign Mission Society was organized and was followed, six years later, by the creation of the Woman's American Baptist Home Mission Society.

Helen Barrett Montgomery, who served as a president of the Woman's

TAKE MY HAND, I'M A STRANGER in PARADISE!

Most women's groups began by starting and maintaining missionary endeavors!
—FRIAR TUCK

American Baptist Foreign Missionary Society, was the first woman to translate the Greek New Testament into modern English and the first woman to be elected president of the Northern Baptist Convention (1921–22). She also helped initiate what later became known as the World Day of Prayer for missions, and she was an aggressive advocate of world missions.

The three decades following the Civil War brought the organization of a women's missionary auxiliary in dozens of denominations, often over the strong opposition of male leaders, but always with the central emphasis on missions.

On several occasions a new women's organization was created because the earlier missionary society insisted its sole focus was on *foreign* missions. One example of that came in 1880 when The Methodist Episcopal Church created the Woman's Home Missionary Society to respond to needs that the Woman's Foreign Missionary Society would not support.

Another example of a response by women to a specific need resulted in the creation in 1886 by the Methodist Episcopal Church, South, of the Woman's Parsonage and

Home Mission Society. That church had grown so rapidly that many preachers did not have a parsonage. The new organization helped finance the construction of 550 parsonages in its first eight years of existence.

As the decades slipped by, however, that central emphasis on missions began to be eroded as other concerns were added to the agenda of the women's organization including Bible study, preparing and serving meals, fellowship, mutual support, feminist issues, and helping pay the preacher.

This evolution can be illustrated by comparing three statements of purpose from the women's organizations in the Christian Church (Disciples of Christ).

The 1874 constitution of the Women's Board of Missions included this statement: "To cultivate a missionary spirit; to encourage mission effort in the church; to disseminate missionary intelligence; and to secure systematic contributions for the missionary work of the Christian Women's Board of Missions."

Each of the four phrases in that statement of purpose was built around missions.

By 1949 this statement of purpose had been revised and abbreviated. It now read, "To develop all women in Christian living and Christian service as a part of the witnessing church of Jesus Christ."

A more recent version came out in 1973 and states the purpose of the Christian Women's Fellowship to be "to provide opportunities for spiritual growth, enrichment, education and creative ministries to enable women to develop a sense of personal responsibility for the whole mission of the Church of Jesus Christ."

Another example of this debate over purpose came when United Methodists concluded that denomination needed an advocacy agency on behalf of women. Instead of assigning that responsibility to the United Methodist Women or to the General Board of Church and Society, the General Conference of 1972 created a new Commission on the Role and Status of Women. Sixteen years later some of the women who had urged creation of that special agency called for its dissolution and a reallocation of that $2 million expenditure every quadrennium to other needs. Their minority report to dissolve that agency was defeated by the narrow vote of 482 to 460.

OF COURSE, SHE'S CARING... BUT WHO CARES ABOUT HER?

TOTALLY FOR OTHERS

Are our women's groups primarily for missions, social advocacy, or to meet the needs of their members?
—FRIAR JUCK

While this was never stated directly, the vote could be read as a decision that the United Methodist Women was not or should not be seen as the advocacy agency on behalf of women. The closeness of that vote, however, does reveal the complexity of this question about purpose. Perhaps a better statement of the issue would be this threefold question, Should the women's organization in your congregation or denomination be organized *primarily* around missions or *primarily* as an advocacy group on behalf of women or *primarily* to be responsive to a variety of the needs of today's women?

One reason this is such an urgent issue is that it introduces a second policy question.

How Broad Is the Umbrella?

Experience suggests that a focus on missions today will not attract as many women as a broader umbrella that includes a variety of concerns. Defining the primary role of the women's organization as a social protest movement usually will attract an even smaller number of adherents.

This means that another way of stating the first policy question is the choice between including a large number of women or concentrating on either missions or social justice as the primary reason for being.

The Women's Missionary Union in the Southern Baptist

WE ALWAYS GET A BETTER VIEW WHEN WE LOOK BEYOND OURSELVES!

Are we willing to broaden our base to attract more members?

—FRIAR TUCK

Convention is an outstanding example of a women's organization centered on missions. Out of the 14.5 million baptized members in that denomination, slightly under 1.2 million were carried as members in 1987 including 173,500 age 5 and under in Mission Friends, 227,000 age 6-11 in Girls in Action, 110,000 age 12-17 in Acteens, and 77,000 in Baptist Young Women. That means approximately 600,000 women, age 30 and over, are members out of an estimated 5 million women, age 30 and over, in the Southern Baptist Convention. That is not a high proportion.

The United Methodist Women report 1.2 million members, most of whom are past 30 years of age, out of nearly 4 million women, age 30 and over, in that denomination. The WMU enlists approximately 12 percent of the women, age 30 and over, in an organization built around missions. The Methodists report approximately one-fourth of all women, age 30 and over, are members of local women's organizations built around a combination of missions, study, projects, fellowship, mutual support, and congregational activities. (It should be mentioned that part of this gap between 12 percent and 26 percent is a reflection of the differences in the definition of the word "member.")

In 1985, the year before the merger that created a new denomination, the membership of the women's organization in The Lutheran Church in America was 212,000 or equivalent to approximately 22 percent of the women in that denomination age 30 and over.

The basic generalization illustrated here is that a narrow

emphasis on missions probably will attract fewer women than a broad and multi-focused organization. Unless an aggressive effort is made, however, to broaden the total program and to reach new generations of women, it is unlikely that any women's organization will be able to attract more than one-third of all the adult women from a particular congregation as regular participants. The difference between 10 percent and 33 percent probably will reflect the decision on purpose and the implementation of that decision.

THE ANSWER: THEY LEAD IN EVANGELISM, FUND-RAISING, MUTUAL SUPPORT and ADULT EDUCATION! THE QUESTION IS...

Are women's organizations an obsolete concept in our day?

—FRIAR TUCK

Is This an Obsolete Concept?

For some critics of the relevance of a women's organization in contemporary society, the first policy question to be addressed is simply, Is this an obsolete concept? Does a need exist for an all-female organization in the churches today? Has the move toward an egalitarian society eliminated the justification that existed a hundred years ago when both congregations and denominations were governed by adult males?

Those who agree that this is an obsolete concept probably should not and will not read this book. A simple response is the women's organization has been, is, and probably will continue to be a distinctive part of the organizational life that can respond to a variety of needs that otherwise will be overlooked. As long as congregations recognize and affirm the differences among people, the need for distinctive special purpose organizations will be heard.

Note: "Irrelevance is one of the directional signs on the road to oblivion!"
—FRIAR TUCK

The caution sign in this discussion, however, is clear and should not be ignored. In thousands of congregations one of the big reasons behind the declining membership in the women's organization has been the creation under a different umbrella of new classes, groups, clubs, and task forces to meet the needs of a new generation of younger women. Irrelevance is one of the directional signs on the road to oblivion!

Movement or Formal Organization?

Perhaps the most complex of these policy questions concerns the difference between the life of a movement and the nurturing of a formal organization.

Most of the predecessor organizations formed during the nineteenth century began as movements. They displayed the almost universal characteristics of a social movement. These include (1) a single clause that the followers believe is the most important issue in their lives, (2) an inspiring and effective leader, ideally with a long tenure, and (3) that single cause becomes a powerful rallying point to attract new members. A fourth, but a far from universal characteristic of a movement, is the identification of a common enemy.[1] For many of the women's missionary movements in the nineteenth century the common enemy was the male leadership of that denomination. That opposition often was a significant asset in launching the movement that evolved into a women's missionary group.

Space prevents calling the roll here of all those visionary leaders, but the list includes Emmy Ewald, Helen Barrett Montgomery, Ann "Nancy" Judson, Belle Harris Bennett, Frances E. Willard, Jennie F. Willing, Lottie Moon, Juliette Mather, Isabella Thoburn, Nannie Helen Burroughs, and Lucinda B. Helm.

These were only a few of the women leaders who created missionary movements in the nineteenth century.

In the beginning, many women's groups were often galvanized by their common opposition to men!

—FRIAR TUCK

The critical question for today is, Do you see your women's group as a movement built around a cause and an inspiring leader? Or do you see it as a formal organization built around purpose, goals, procedures, changing priorities, and program?

That is a huge difference, and a radically different approach is needed for the revitalization of a formal organization than is appropriate for launching a new era for what now appears to be a weary and goalless movement.

The power of program is always greater than the most powerful personality!

FRIAR TUCK

WHEREVER TWO OR THREE ARE GATHERED, A LOT OF FOLKS ARE MISSING!

What once worked so well in smaller congregations may not be appropriate for today's larger churches!

—FRIAR TUCK

Organization or Federation of Groups?

One of the most fundamental structural questions reflects the difference between two radically different approaches. One is to create a single-purpose organization and expect every member's primary loyalty to be to that organization (or movement). This was the approach followed by missionary societies that began as movements. It is an appropriate approach for a movement. It also is a comfortable structure for smaller churches.

One of the big changes on the ecclesiastical scene since 1890, however, is that the average size of Protestant congregations is nearly triple what it was a hundred years ago. The structure that worked so well in smaller congregations for decades may not be appropriate for the larger congregations of today.

A second structural approach is to create a large "general" women's organization that is subdivided into several "circles" or groups. Many of the members will express their primary loyalty to a circle, not to the larger organization. This is a widely used approach today and removes the ceiling on size. A reasonable goal is to organize one circle for every fifty adult women in the congregation. If the circle averages 15 to 17 members, it may achieve the goal of including approximately one-third of all adult women as active members of the women's organization.

These are two radically different approaches! Each has advantages. It is easier to keep the focus on a single reason for being, such as missions, in the unitary structure, but that usually works best with a long-tenured, dedicated, and highly competent leader.

The second structural approach usually will include a larger number of women and be responsive to a greater variety of needs, but will require a larger number of capable leaders. In the first approach the continuity is largely in that meaningful cause and in that dedicated leader. In the second approach much of the continuity is in the organizational structure, traditions, customs, goals, and the fellowship ties that members have with one another in a particular circle.

In the first, the primary loyalties of the members are to the cause and to that leader. In the second, for many women, the primary loyalty is to a circle and/or a group of friends.

Which approach do you plan to follow?

The Place in That Congregation?

A sixth policy question looks to a larger context. How does the women's organization fit into the life and ministry of this worshiping community? Is it simply one of several small face-to-face groups? Is it one organization in a congregation built largely around organizations including a men's fellowship, the choir program, a youth group, a set of administrative committees, the Sunday school, and the weekday program for preschool children? Or is it an auxiliary that is outside the basic structure of congregational life? Is the *primary* tie to the governing board of that congregation? Or to the denominational women's organization?

The choice among those three alternatives usually will influence (1) the relationship to the pastor, (2) the degree of autonomy in program planning and decision making, (3) the allocation of funds gathered by the women's organization, (4) the procedure to be followed in choosing new officers, (5) the receptivity to innovation, (6) the requirements for membership, (7) the relationships with the missions committee, the Sunday school, and the ministry of music, (8) the place of corporate worship in the women's organization's meetings, (9) the priorities determining the allocation of members' time and energy, and (10) the "promotion ladder" for the leaders.

Large or Small Groups?

Overlapping these last three policy questions is one that is widely ignored in practice. This grows out of the huge differences between the dynamics of small groups and the most effective management of large groups.

While this greatly oversimplifies an extremely complex subject, groups may be divided into four categories according to size. A huge body of research suggests that small groups begin to lose some of those many advantages that are a part of small group dynamics when the size exceeds seven participants.[2]

A distinctively different type of group begins to emerge when the number of members ranges between eight and sixteen or seventeen. If sufficient reinforcing factors are at work, these can be seen as "overgrown" small groups. These reinforcing factors may include the presence of kinship ties, the fact that the members of that group see one another at least a couple of times every week, a clearly agreed upon and nondivisive agenda for when they meet, refreshments, friendship ties, the long tenure of most of the participants in that group, and a common world view. Many adult Sunday school classes and circles in women's organizations benefit from several of these reinforcing factors. Middle-sized groups consist of those with about seventeen to thirty-five or forty regular participants. These groups usually benefit from the presence of competent leadership, friendship ties, a specific and clearly defined assignment or task, a schedule with clearly stated beginning and closing times that are followed, an attractive rallying point or project, the use of name tags in the absence of existing friendship or kinship ties, a faster pace during the meetings, laughter, visual communication, refreshments including a wide choice of beverages, and a maximum of ninety minutes between breaks. The chancel choir or the large adult class built around an attractive teacher are common examples.

The fourth category consists of the large groups that exceed forty participants. As a general rule, the larger the number of participants, the more influential is the role of the leader, the greater the need for close observance of the schedule, the more beneficial is singing, and the more important a redundant system for reinforcing cohesion. The difficulty of building and maintaining large groups is one reason why so few chancel choirs average more than forty to forty-five voices on Sunday morning[3] and why one-fourth of all Protestant congregations average fewer than forty at Sunday morning worship.

A common practice among women's organizations has been to assign twenty to thirty-five women to one group or circle, use a system that is appropriate for small or overgrown small groups to manage that circle, and to deplore the fact that attendance at the monthly meeting rarely exceeds fifteen or sixteen women.

The policy question that emerges from this discussion is one of internal consistency. What is the number of participants we will recommend for each circle and will we offer guidelines appropriate for that size group?

One of the more common experiences with internal inconsistency is to invite seventy-five to a hundred women to the monthly "general" meeting, utilize a system that is appropriate for middle-sized groups, and be disappointed when the attendance is between thirty-five and forty. If large group meetings are to be encouraged, the denominational agency should provide congregational leaders with the guidelines appropriate for planning and managing large group events.

Tenure Versus Performance

A concept called "the learning curve" suggests a surgeon will be more skilled, display a higher level of self-confidence, and take less time in performing a specific surgical procedure for the fifty-third time than will be displayed the first time that surgeon performs that particular operation. The same generalization applies to building a bookcase, writing a book, changing a tire on an automobile, milking a cow, or serving as president of the women's fellowship.

One tradeoff is between experience, skill, and performance on the one hand and the goal of "passing the job around," enlisting new leaders, and minimizing institutional stagnation. How long do you believe the term of office should be for the president of the women's fellowship in a parish? For chairing the board of the regional judicatory? For chairing the executive committee of the national women's organization? Is two years insufficient time to reach the peak of that learning curve? What is the ideal term of office?

A second tradeoff is between the power of paid staff and the power of the volunteer officers. The longer the tenure of the volunteer, the less likely paid staff will dominate the organization. The shorter the tenure of volunteer officers, the easier it is for paid staff to control priorities, goals, and the agenda. The longer the tenure of volunteer officers, the more likely the partially paranoid members will suspect the existence of an unholy alliance between staff and volunteer leaders.

These generalizations apply to both congregational and denominational leaders.

Attracting New Members

For several decades nearly all the women's fellowships depended largely on four sources for new members as that initial parade of dedicated women grew older, disappeared, and were replaced by newcomers. The first and most powerful was the attraction of the cause. For nearly two centuries missions has been, and continues to be, the most attractive rallying point in American Protestantism. Some will argue that the attractiveness of missions as a rallying point peaked in the 1850–1960 era. History may validate that position, but a huge amount of evidence exists to support the contention that missions is still the most powerful rallying point on the American religious scene.

A second source was the attraction of that dedicated leadership. A third was inherited institutional loyalties as daughters followed in the footsteps of their mothers. The fourth was denominational loyalties that aroused support for whatever program that denomination advocated.

The generations born after 1940 clearly did not inherit institutional loyalties from their parents as the generations born in the first four decades of the twentieth century inherited institutional loyalties from their parents. This can be seen in the records of political parties, the old-line Protestant denominations, the student body of private colleges and universities, American automobile manufacturers, the Roman Catholic Church, service clubs, veterans' organizations, Scouting, and private clubs for women as well as in the women's organizations in the churches.

The Women's Organization
OFFICE OF ASSIMILATION

SHE'S BEING CALLED
TO A CAUSE!

—FRIAR TUCK

"You know you belong
when you know
you are needed."

Likewise denominational loyalties have been seriously eroded during the second half of the twentieth century. The most obvious example is that a huge number of people who were reared in Catholic, Methodist, Presbyterian, Lutheran, Episcopal, Baptist, and other denominationally related congregations are now attending independent churches—often without benefit of a letter of transfer.

The obvious policy question that emerges from this discussion is what will be done to attract a new generation of members? That is the theme of the last section of this book, but two old adages offer direction. The first is, "You know you belong when you know you are needed." One example is the welcome accorded the new tenor by the choir. The second adage is, "New groups for new people." While a few newcomers are content to join long-established groups, many more gain a sense of belonging by helping pioneer the new. That is one reason why new church development must receive a high priority by any denomination seeking to include the new immigrants from Latin America or Asia or seeking to reach the generations born after 1955.

Exclusionary or Inclusionary?

Overlapping this last point is another widely ignored issue. This is the distinction between organizing groups around inclusionary principles versus using exclusionary principles. When a group is organized around fellowship and/or study, it quickly becomes exclusionary. This has nothing to do with the members of the group. It is simply a fact of life. The closely knit family organized around love, caring for one another, and fellowship that includes the mother, father, a seven-year-old, a five-year-old, and a two-year-old can boast of its closeness. When mother brings a new baby home from the hospital, however, that two-year-old probably will display exclusionary characteristics. Most universities close registration for classes after the second week of school each quarter or semester. One of the reasons the German army held on so long in 1944 was because they did not attempt to send replacements into frontline companies. One of the reasons for the disaster American armies encountered in Vietnam was the policy of rotating officers after six months of combat duty and rotating enlisted men after one year.[4] American Protestantism is filled with thousands of examples of congregations organized around a common nationality and language heritage, fellowship, nostalgia, worship, and the sacraments that are unable to accept newcomers from a different nationality heritage.

If circles in a women's organization are organized around fellowship, study, nostalgia, and verbal skills, one should not be surprised when they fail to attract sufficient replacements to maintain the size of that group.

The policy question that is raised is, Will circles be organized around exclusionary principles or around inclusionary principles? This can be a self-fulfilling prophecy type of issue.

The Legitimacy of Money-Raising Events?

One of the more controversial issues in women's organizations in the churches is the legitimacy of bazaars, dinners, garage sales, auctions, craft fairs, and other money-raising activities. Should they be barred, tolerated, or encouraged? The potentialities of money-raising events will be discussed later, but the policy question to be raised here is based on the assumption that money-raising events can provide an attractive entry point for the enlistment and assimilation of new members. Therefore, if money-raising activities are discouraged or barred, what will be substituted as attractive entry points for new members?

Do You Believe in Generational Theory?

Do you encourage each group or circle to be an intergenerational mix of women? Or do you believe that people prefer to socialize with those from their own age cohort? Considerable evidence can be mobilized in support of the contention that each generation of Americans share several common, but not universal characteristics.[5] On the other hand, many leaders are convinced it is good for people to work and socialize with different generations.

What do you believe should be the dominant assumption in creating circles in the women's organization? Should they be multi-generational? Or should each circle draw most or all of its members from the same generation?

Experience suggests many benefits can be derived by creating multi-generational circles, but the number of participants will be smaller. Which side of that tradeoff do you support?

How Central Is Worship?

One of the evolutionary changes in many women's fellowships has been from Bible study and prayer at every meeting to asking someone to prepare a brief devotional message to a full-scale corporate worship experience. Today it is not unusual for the monthly or quarterly "general" meeting, as well as for many denominational gatherings, to include a twenty-five-to-fifty-minute worship experience including the singing of hymns, readings from the Holy Scriptures, a period of intercessory prayer, a sermon, perhaps an offering and, far more frequently today than in the 1950s, Holy Communion.

Why this has happened is a matter of speculation, but it does raise an important policy question.

When the women's missionary society was organized solely around missions, it was perceived by many men as a rival to both the congregation and to the denomination. Eventually, however, nearly everyone recognized that the challenge of missions was so vast there was room for both congregational and denominational missionary enterprises, plus whatever might be initiated by the women. When measured in terms of missionaries and money, the women often surpassed the efforts of the rest of that denomination, but a cooperative relationship could be maintained.

While the emphasis may vary, nearly every Christian congregation is organized around bringing people together for the corporate worship of God. If the corporate worship of God becomes either the central organizing principle of the women's organization in a local church, or even one of the two or three most attractive aspects of the women's group, will it be reasonable to expect that a cooperative relationship can be attained with the pastor, the rest of the congregation, and the denomination?

The parallel that may merit consideration is the adult Sunday school class which meets at 9:30 A.M. every Sunday morning. That hour often includes a hymn, an offering for the support of "our missionary project," readings from the Bible, prayer, a meditation, a closing hymn, and the bene-diction.

Someone walking up the sidewalk to attend the eleven o'clock worship service may encounter an acquaintance who is a member of that class and obviously headed toward the parking lot. "Aren't you going to church today?" is the greeting.

"Already bin," replies the member of that adult class as he continues on his way to the parking lot. At least a few preachers find this to be a disturbing occurrence.

How central do you see corporate worship to be to the future of the women's organization in your congregation?

The Role of the Pastor

For several decades male pastors often perceived the women's fellowship as "Off Limits for Men!" Does your pastor see it as a competitor for the affections and loyalty of a group of members (sometimes even including the member married to that pastor) or as a loyal work crew to whom unpleasant chores could be delegated or as a valuable ally in promoting missions or as a minor league farm club useful in training future congregational leaders ("Every other year we choose the outgoing president of the women's association to become the moderator and on alternate years we select a man") or as a source of funds for emergency needs not covered by the budget or as the victims for the pastor's annual Bible study or as a program agency or as a completely independent, self-governing, self-propagating, and self-financing organization or as a source of future-oriented and skilled allies for implementing one of the pastor's new ideas?

What do you believe should be the ideal relationship between the women's fellowship and the pastor? How can you encourage the building of that relationship? Can that be institutionalized so a new pastor will find it easy to fit into that relationship? Will it make any difference if the next pastor is a woman?

Women Only?

One of the questions raised periodically of those who write the advice columns for the newspapers concerns the maximum age for the boy who accompanies his mother to the public women's rest room. The usual answer is age three or four or five.

A parallel question for the women's fellowship is whether it is and will continue to be exclusively a female organization. One response is, "That's a ridiculous question! By definition it is an all-female organization."

Another response is based on the old adage, "Find a need and fill it." If the congregation does not offer attractive choices for the young childless couple or the retired couple

who want to spend their discretionary time together, not in separate groups, should the women's organization create a new group in response to new needs?

This can be a critical policy issue for those interested in (a) increasing the numerical size of the women's fellowship and/or (b) reaching the generation of adults born after 1955. One alternative is to conclude, "No, we don't do that," and watch other groups and organizations in that congregation attract the interest and participation of a new generation of younger couples. The second alternative is to affirm coed circles.

Those who see this as a far-out issue should note that in scores of congregations men now contribute much of what is sold at the annual bazaar to raise money for missions. Should men be asked to contribute their handicrafts, but not have a voice on how those dollars will be allocated? (This issue will be discussed in the next to last section of the concluding chapter of this book.)

What Is That Relationship?

One of the more divisive policy questions concerns the relationship of the women's organization to the organizational structure of the denomination. A second facet of this question concerns the relationship between the local group and the denominational agency.

Most of the women's organizations that trace their origins back to their days as a missionary society were created as auxiliaries. As self-governing, self-financing, and self-propagating agencies these early organizations enjoyed a high degree of independence. In several cases their tie to the denomination was tenuous. For many that denominational tie was reinforced largely by the tremendous denominational loyalty of the leaders—despite the way some of the male clergy treated them. The twentieth century brought a series of efforts to transform these missionary auxiliaries into departments within the denominational structure. One of the earliest came in 1906 when women in the Southern branch of Methodism discovered the bishops had made a unilateral decision to reorganize the women's work and in 1910 the home and foreign missionary agencies were combined into a single unit.

While it is impossible to prove a cause-and-effect relationship, this structural integration of the women's organization into the denominational system eventually was often followed by (a) a diffusion or blurring of the centrality of missions as the primary purpose of the women's organization, (b) a reduction (after allowances are made for inflation) in the amount of money raised by women for missions, (c) an aging of the membership, (d) an erosion of the vigor, vitality, and enthusiasm, and (e) limited success in attracting new generations of younger women as new members.

This organizational integration usually was supported by arguments for efficiency, economy, coordination, better internal communication, a unified witness on the mission field, elimination of the duplication of effort, reduction of the sense of competition, a holistic view of ministry, and improved accountability.

Although other factors enter into this debate, the historical record suggests that the women's organization will be more likely to thrive, to resist the subversion of goals, and to fulfill its original purpose if it is not a structural part of the denominational bureaucracy.

This will not surprise any student of bureaucratic organizations. The separate self-governing, self-financing, and self-propagating single function agency is far more likely than a bureaucratic structure to (a) resist turning a means-to-an-end

WE LOVE OUR DENOMINATION, BUT OUR GROUPS WON'T GROW IF OUR PRIORITIES ARE OUT OF OUR CONTROL!

DENOMINATIONAL LOYALTY

—FRIAR TUCK

into an end, (b) adhere to its original purpose, (c) spark and support creativity, (d) raise money, (e) attract new supporters, (f) recruit new and competent leadership, (g) not be diverted by internal bureaucratic struggles for power, (h) be sensitive and responsive to the needs of an ever-changing world, (i) adapt to the needs of a new clientele, and (j) be able to attract self-motivated volunteers.

Do you prefer the women's organization in your denomination to be a department in the denominational structure or to function as a separate self-governing auxiliary?

A second part of this issue raises the question about the relationships of the local units. Is their primary tie to the congregation? Or is the primary tie to the women's organization in that regional judicatory? Who determines policies, formulates priorities, suggests new programs, defines the guidelines, and relates the work of that local unit to the larger church? To whom is that local unit accountable? To the governing board of that congregation? To itself? To God and only God? To the regional judicatory? To the pastor? To the leaders of the national women's organization?

The most frequent response by male congregational leaders to those and similar questions clearly is a product of fear, intimidation, cowardice, faintheartedness, survival instincts, and, perhaps, even terror, rather than a desire to promote efficiency, economy, good internal communication, and coordination in programming and outreach. This reluctance often is explained by statements such as, "We already have enough battles to fight without taking on the women."

Despite this widespread evasion of the issue, the question still remains whether the local units should give a high priority to enhancing the sense of denominational allegiance within that congregation.

Finally, the question must be raised, Were the regional and national agencies created to serve the congregational women's fellowship? Or are the local units expected to follow the mandates and accept the priorities coming from national and/or regional agencies? If this is a team, to use an old farm analogy, who is the lead horse?

Missions or Evangelism?

Traditionally missions was the most common reason for creating a separate women's organization. Traditionally most churches have drawn a distinction between missions and evangelism or the recruitment of new members for congregations.

Although it rarely was a stated goal, hundreds of congregations discovered that the women's fellowship was one of its most attractive entry points for new members. The high quality of the teaching ministry, the emphasis on missions and outreach, the bazaars, the opportunities for "hands on" involvement in doing ministry, and the need for more volunteers created a wide open door. Many women first joined the women's fellowship and eventually united with that worshiping congregation.

Should the women's organization in your church aggressively reach out to people who are not actively involved in the life of any worshiping community and invite them to join a circle or to help create a new group in response to newly emerging needs? Or is that not an appropriate role for the women's organization? Should the primary focus be on involving women who already are members of that congregation? In several denominations the constitution or bylaws make it very clear one must become a member of that congregation before being eligible to become an officer of that women's fellowship or a delegate to denominational meetings. This is consistent with the view of the women's

fellowship as a program department of that parish. It is not consistent with the view of the women's fellowship as a self-governing and self-propagating auxiliary nor with any effort to make the women's effort a significant entry point for new people into that parish. It also overlooks the fact that at least 3 million women today see themselves as active weekly participants in the life of two different congregations.

The Growing Number
of Bequests

Recent decades have changed the most common synonym for "poor" from "elderly" to "single parent mother" and "child." Recent decades have seen the number of bequests received by churches triple in twenty years. Today close to one-third of all accumulated wealth is owned by persons past age sixty-five. Today many mature women feel a closer tie to that local women's fellowship than they do to that congregation or to the current pastor or to the denomination.

Should the leaders in the local women's organization cultivate this relationship and encourage members to remember the women's fellowship in their wills? If so, should the women's organization create a separate nonprofit legal corporation to receive these bequests? Or should members be encouraged to leave the bequest to the congregation, but with restrictions on the use of both the legacy and on the income from the investments? Should all income be designated for missions? Or should the congregation be allowed (encouraged?) to use the income from these bequests for the operating budget? Or only for capital improvements?[6]

Once again the question must be asked, What if it works? What happens if the women's fellowship in that three-hundred-member congregation is the recipient or trustee of a million dollars or more in bequests? Would that create diversionary or divisive problems?

What is your response to this policy question?

The Place of Issues

Potentially the most divisive policy question facing the leaders of women's organizations in the churches is the priority to be given to issue-centered ministries. How much time, energy, leadership, money, and other resources should be devoted to issues such as abortion, the ordination of avowed homosexual seminary graduates, nuclear power, prohibition, euthansia, the legalization of the sale of marijuana and cocaine, the equal rights amendment, taxing Social Security benefits, disarmament, human rights in Africa, vouchers for parents of school-age children, American foreign policy, easy access to birth control devices for teenagers, elimination of the death penalty, control of pornography or legalization of the over-the-counter sale of the abortifacient RU 486? What proportion of the agenda should be devoted to these and other issues?

Three generalizations offer a context for this discussion. The first is missions usually can be a broad umbrella and an attractive rallying point for bringing large numbers of Christians together. This generalization applies to denominations, congregations, adult Sunday school classes, and the women's organization. Missions was the cause that brought many of the original women's organizations into existence.

The other side of that generalization is that while any one issue can be an appealing rallying point for bringing like-minded people together, a long-term focus on issues can be divisive as new issues are added to the agenda. A magnificent series of interfaith coalitions of Catholics, Protestants, and Jews was created in the 1960s in support of the civil rights movement. Subsequently, these coalitions were torn apart by such divisive issues as abortion, free access by high school students to birth control aids, and the municipal "gay rights" ordinance.

It is difficult to build a permanent coalition around issue centered ministries. What some may see as a just cause others see in an entirely different light. Most Christians probably would agree that a call for stricter regulation of pornography should and would be a unifying rallying point that would not be divisive. One public opinion analyst reported, however, that the division between men and women on that issue was the greatest he had ever seen on any question that classified public opinion polls by gender.[7] It also is one of the most divisive issues among women.

The passage of time also changes people's opinion on issues. In 1948 the "liberal Protestant" position was to oppose federal aid to public schools. Twenty-five years later the liberal Protestant position called for increased federal aid to public schools.[8]

During the last years of the nineteenth century the liberal position was to oppose the efforts of corporations such as the Prudential Life Insurance Company, the Metropolitan Life Insurance Company, and the John Hancock Company to sell lower-class parents life insurance policies on their children. By 1902 over three million children were insured. This was interpreted by many church leaders as immoral. The typical premium was three cents a week, but by the 1920s it was up to a dime a week for the more expensive policies. Newspapers denounced this as an incentive for parents to murder their children. Clergymen, social workers, physicians, and other crusaders urged state legislatures to prohibit this system that would reward parents for the death of a child.

By 1910, as more middle-class parents began to take out life insurance policies on their children, this began to be viewed as a prudent, commendable, and desirable practice and won the support of an increasing number of the liberal molders of public opinion.[9] Today few see the insurance of the lives of children as a sinful action.

A second generalization is that if the decision is made to concentrate on issue-centered ministries, it might be wiser to conceptualize the women's organization as a movement built around a cause and led by inspiring leaders, rather than as a formal organization. Movements can thrive as single issue groups, but organizations can be torn apart if the focus is on issues. A recent example of this was the bland platform of the Democratic Party in 1988, which was designed, unlike the platforms of 1980 and 1984, to build unity and broaden the support base, rather than to advance a cause—and helped lose an election.

A third generalization concerns the basic approach to issue-centered ministries. From a congregational perspective it may be wiser, less divisive, and more effective to create a series of single focus task forces, each with its own leadership and its own issue, rather than to try to lodge in one organization, such as the women's fellowship, the primary responsibility to serve as that congregation's conscience on the social justice agenda. It also may be wise to consider allowing men to

THE DENOMINATION OFTEN HAS MORE THAN OUR HEARTS ON HOLD!

Can we continue to feed the organization at the risk of starving its members?

— FRIAR TUCK

have a role in issue centered ministries rather than assigning that to the women's organization.

Organizational Goals or Needs of People?

The last of these twenty policy questions also overlaps a few of the earlier ones directed at the natural tendency in any long-established organization to focus on the needs of the organization rather than the needs of people.[10]

The best contemporary example of that is the contrast between many large and rapidly growing congregations that concentrate their resources on responding to the religious needs of the people and that huge number of long-established and numerically declining churches that place a high priority on enlisting people to help fulfill congregational and/or denominational goals.

For leaders in the women's organization this often comes down to a simple either-or question. Which is the more urgent priority? To seek and include large numbers of women? Or to follow the denominational guidelines and work toward accomplishing the organizational goals with a smaller number of participants?

A simple, but very significant example is the question, Should we require every circle to follow the same format and to study the same material, or should we form one or two new circles for younger "born-again" women and/or for self-identified charismatic Christians where the focus will be largely on one's own personal and religious journey?

The second alternative in that choice may (1) attract more younger women, (2) not be consistent with the guidelines, (3) disturb some of the longtime loyal members, (4) represent a deviation from the focus on missions, (5) threaten the pastor, (6) raise questions in the minds of several congregational leaders who see this as going beyond the traditional boundaries of the women's fellowship, (7) produce several highly motivated, enthusiastic, and committed candidates when the time comes to seek new leaders, (8) upset some of the leaders in denominational headquarters, (9) introduce a new generation of younger members into that congregation, and (10) cause some of the longtime members to leave the circle they have been in for years to join one of these new circles.

In other words, it is impossible to do only one thing. Every action may have unanticipated consequences.

This question represents a major fork in the road for those local units that have experienced difficulty in attracting women born after 1945. While many exceptions do exist, the generations born after 1945 are far more likely to be found in churches that focus on their religious needs. They tend to ignore the churches that concentrate on organizational goals. The generations born before 1940 are far more numerous in those churches that focus on organizational goals, but in part that may be the product of lethargy, institutional loyalties, friendship and kinship ties, inertia and endurance rather than active support for those organizational goals.[11]

Which of these twenty policy questions do you believe are the most crucial for the women's fellowship in your congregation? For the leaders of the denominationally related women's organization? Who will place these questions on the agenda? How will they be resolved? Will the answers to the several questions be internally consistent with one another? Can you secure agreement on the tradeoffs?

Internally consistent answers to these policy questions will enable today's leaders to offer direction, will provide a conceptual framework for setting priorities, and will influence the numerical growth or decline of your women's organization. The answers to these questions also will provide a useful context for reflecting on points raised in the rest of this book.

Two Scenarios

"I can't understand why so many of our younger women fail to recognize and accept their obligations," reflected May Woodward as she met with six other women one Tuesday morning in January. This was scheduled as the first of three planning meetings for these seven women who served as the executive committee of the Women's Fellowship at Trinity Church. The program year for the Women's Fellowship runs from July 1 to June 30 and the executive committee always presents to the general meeting in April the proposed program for the coming year. By the end of their March meeting these seven women expected to be ready to offer a series of specific recommendations for the coming year.

"My mother taught me that everyone has responsibilities in this world and the Women's Fellowship is a special responsibility of every woman in this church," continued the gentle sixty-four-year-old May Woodward who was completing the second year of her two-year term as president of the Women's Fellowship.

May had been nominated and elected two years earlier for this two-year term because (a) she had never served as president and several felt she had been slighted inasmuch as at least seven other women had served as president on two separate occasions—May was due this honor, (b) the other women admired her deep commitment to missions, (c) she had been a member of this Women's Fellowship for over forty years, (d) no one else would accept the nomination, (e) May had served as a circle leader, secretary, missions chairperson, treasurer, and vice-president in previous years and knew the organization, (f) her mother had been one of the three or four most effective leaders in the history of this women's organization which demonstrated May had good bloodlines, (g) everyone loved and respected the gentle and dedicated May, (h) for decades people had referred to May as a model of a loving and committed Christian, and (i) she deeply believed in the value of the Women's Fellowship.

"I've been in this church all my life and I never questioned my obligation to become a member of the Women's Fellowship as soon as I turned twenty-one," she explained.

"I was brought up the same way," agreed the sixty-nine-year-old, loyal and hardworking Vera Heath. "My grandmother helped organize the first Women's Missionary Society in this church. My mother followed in her footsteps and expected me to follow in hers. I must add that for my mother the Women's Fellowship ranked right up there just below God with her family and the church as one of the three most important things in her life. She enjoyed working in it, missions was almost an obsession with her, nearly all of her friends were in the Fellowship, and when she was terminally ill, they generously gave their time to help take care of her during those last few weeks before she died. A week before she died, she asked me to bring her the dress she wanted to be buried in to make sure her life member Women's Fellowship pin was pinned on it in the right place."

"That duplicates the story of my mother," recalled Evelyn Harrison, a widow for nearly twenty years and a dedicated member. "The Women's Fellowship was central to her life. My father traveled for a living and was home only on weekends. The Fellowship made up for his being gone so much. I feel that if my mother had been born sixty years later, she might have gone to seminary and become a minister, but of course that was completely out of the question for her generation."

"I guess you all know our daughter-in-law is a minister," commented May Woodward proudly. "I had always hoped one of our three boys would hear the call and go into the ministry, but none did. However, after graduating from the university, our second son, who is an accountant, started

LEARNING TO PREACH WAS EASY, THEY ALREADY UNDERSTOOD CARING AND COMPASSION!

Women have gone from being caretakers and homemakers to becoming preacher-creatures!
—FRIAR TUCK☺

going to a small church in the town where he had found a job. He fell in love with the preacher, got married, and now has two wonderful children. Because good accountants are in short supply nearly everywhere, he has been what they now call the trailing spouse in that marriage. She's now the pastor of a real good church in Pennsylvania. Both children are now teenagers and they love to brag about their mother being a minister."

"We have four daughters," announced the shy Lois Richards in what resembled a "keeping-up-with-the-Jones" tone. "One is an architect, one is a lawyer, the third is a department head with a big insurance company in Jacksonville, and the fourth is a homemaker with three beautiful children, but they live nearly six hundred miles from here, so we don't see those grandchildren as often as we would like."

"You two have just identified the big reasons why we have so much trouble appealing to younger women to become active in the Fellowship," interrupted the outspoken Harriet O'Brien, who rarely waited for people to ask for her opinion. "Today women can do anything they want, and they gain fulfillment out of their work. Our mothers faced severe limitations on what they could do outside the home and the church, and so many found fulfillment through their work in the women's organization. That was the only place open to them to express their creativity, to fill a leadership role, and to run their own show. Today our Women's Fellowship has lots of competition for women's talents, skills, time, leadership ability, and energy."

"Yep, that's the heart of the problem," agreed Evelyn Harrison. "Today most of the women work outside the home and there's nobody left to join a women's group. I saw an article in *Time* magazine a couple of years ago that told how women's clubs all across the country are in trouble and their membership has dropped in half during the past thirty years. Back when women had their afternoons free, the clubs flourished, but now all of the women have jobs."[1]

"That's not quite true," corrected the 57-year-old Gertrude Baxter and the youngest member of this group. "I attended a workshop last month where the leader pointed out that back in 1950 there were 26 million women who were not in the labor force and that has increased to 43 million today. So it's not really a shortage of women who aren't working outside the home that's behind our decline."

"I can't believe that," retorted Ethel Beale. "Everybody knows that most of today's women are work-

Item: "Today's women can do anything... they gain fulfillment from their work."
—FRIAR TUCK

Today, we have lots of competition for women's time, talents, and energy!
—FRIAR TUCK

Women's organizations are in direct competition with cars and credit cards!
—FRIAR TUCK

ing. Whoever worked up those numbers must be talking about college students or young mothers on welfare."

"No, that's not the way it is," replied Gertrude as she carefully studied the material in her notebook. "If you admit that for a long time we've drawn most of our members from women who are forty-five or older, that group also has increased in numbers. In 1960 there were 18.4 million American women age forty-five and older who were not in the labor force. By 1989 that group had increased to over 27 million women. In addition, despite all you hear to the contrary, about three out of every ten women who are employed work at a part-time job.[2] The source of our problem is not that all of the women are employed outside the home. We can use that as an excuse, but that's not the real reason we have only half as many women in the Fellowship as we did thirty years ago."

"Well, that may be true," reluctantly conceded Ethel Beale,"but a lot of those women in their fifties and sixties are traveling or their husband has taken early retirement and they've moved to some retirement village in the Sunbelt or something. I don't care what your statistics show, Gertie, I know there aren't as many women out there with the free afternoons as there used to be."

"If you want to see what happened to all of those free afternoons women have," caustically explained the blunt spoken Harriet O'Brien, who enjoyed calling it as she saw it, "go over to the shopping mall any afternoon of the week or drive up and visit that group of outlet stores about sixty miles north of here or take in one of the matinees at that six-screen theater across the street from the shopping mall. I can believe Gertrude's figures. There are more older women out there with free afternoons than was true thirty years ago. The difference is today everyone of them has her own car and credit card!"

"That was one of the points that came up repeatedly in this workshop I attended," affirmed Gertrude Baxter. "The women's organizations in the churches face far more competition for women's time and energy, and institutional loyalties are weaker than they used to be. You can talk all you want, May and Vera and Evelyn, about responsibilities and obligations, but that won't bring a new generation of younger women into this group. If we don't focus on the needs of this new generation of younger women, we're doomed to seeing this group grow older and smaller."

"Well, that leads into the first issue I wanted us to discuss," declared May Woodward as she glanced at her watch and decided it was time to get down to business. "Evelyn here, who is head of the Esther Circle, called me the other day and asked if we could consider merging the Esther Circle with the Martha Circle. Evelyn says they're down to five women and the Martha Circle has only six. What do you think of that? Should we recommend combining those two circles?"

"That's not quite what I said," corrected Evelyn, a vigorous and healthy seventy-nine-year-old who still drove her own car. "I told you we're down to five women who can get out to circle meetings. We still have eleven members, but two are in nursing homes and four others are shutins."

After a few minutes of discussion it was agreed to recommend the merger of these two circles. This would reduce the number of circles from five to four. A decade earlier there had been seven, but a couple of years ago two other circles had merged, and last year one had dissolved when one of the three key members moved to a retirement center a hundred miles away, a second had died, and a third had gone to live in another state with her recently divorced daughter to look after three grandchildren while their mother worked.

"At least a dozen women have come to me urging that we

GULP! I CAN'T SEE AN UPTURN AT THE BOTTOM OF THIS RIDE!

WOMEN'S GROUP

Sadly, to merge circles and eliminate annual events are often acts of desperation not preservation!

—FRIAR TUCK

cancel the bazaar this year," spoke up Ethel Beale. "They say it's too much work for the amount of money we make, and that it would be easier to meet our mission obligations by raising our dues."

"We don't have dues," corrected Vera Heath. "That is a monthly freewill offering."

"Well, call it what you will," continued Ethel, "the women I know are tired of the bazaar and would like us to discontinue it."

"I feel the same way," agreed Evelyn Harrison. "I'm too old to be able to do my share."

After a half hour of discussion, with only Gertrude Baxter dissenting, it was agreed to recommend discontinuance of the annual bazaar.

At the February meeting this group also decided to recommend (a) changing the system of rotating women from one circle to another every other year to make this an annual exercise in order to encourage women to meet and make new friends and to break up what were perceived as "cliques," (b) focusing in on the work of the denomination in Africa as the study emphasis for each of those four circles, (c) accepting the invitation of Bethany Church, a similar sized congregation of another denomination meeting in a building two blocks away, to co-sponsor three bus trips for senior citizens during the coming year, (d) canceling the annual mother-daughter banquet because of poor attendance the past two years, (e) preparing attractive posters to be displayed in the corridors to invite women not now members to join the Women's Fellowship, and (f) appropriating the first two hundred dollars of the new year's receipts to replace broken and missing dishes, silverware, and pans in the church kitchen.

All of these recommendations were perfected, rephrased, and agreed upon at the March meeting of the executive committee. At the April general meeting, attended by thirty-nine women, these recommendations were approved after a brief discussion. That business session also included the presentation of the report of the nominating committee chaired by Gertrude Baxter. A few eyebrows were lifted when Gertie read the name of the sixty-six-year-old Susan Brown as the nominee for the presidency for the coming year, but no one voiced any objection.

Many years earlier Susan had dropped out of college after two years to marry Sam Brown the day after he graduated. Twelve years later Susan was the mother of a ten-year-old son, an eight-year-old daughter, a five-year-old son, and a two-year-old daughter while Sam was climbing the career ladder in a large corporation. During their first twenty-five years of marriage the Browns moved seven times which (a) produced seven promotions for Sam and (b) taught Susan the skills of moving into a new setting, meeting and making new friends, and resolving conflict.

The year Susan turned forty-seven the younger daughter left for college and Susan agreed to the pleas of a neighbor who repeatedly had asked her to come in and run the office of a new business he had launched three years earlier. Twelve years later sixty-one-year-old Sam Brown was given the choice of a promotion that would require an eighth move to another state or an attractive early retirement package. After a long discussion Sam and his fifty-nine-year-old wife agreed to take the retirement option.

They moved here to be near Sam's widowed mother. Susan and Sam golfed, joined Trinity Church where Sam soon became a respected new leader, traveled, looked after Sam's mother, fixed up the sixty-nine-year-old house they had purchased for their retirement years, and met and made many new friends. Four years later, after returning home from a visit to Sam's mother in a nursing home, Susan began to prepare the evening meal while Sam sat down to watch the evening news on television and read the paper. When Susan called him and received no answer, she went into the family room to find Sam in his favorite chair with the newspaper over his face and a game show, which he despised, blaring from the television set. Susan lifted the newspaper, tried to wake her husband, and suddenly realized he might be dead. She telephoned the paramedics who rushed Sam to the hospital where he was pronounced dead on arrival.

Three years later, this sixty-six-year-old widow was elected president of the Women's Fellowship at Trinity Church.

About a year and a half after Sam's death, Gertie Baxter had invited Susan to come to a meeting of her circle. This was the first contact with the women's organization of any church Susan had had in over twenty years. Thirty years and five moves previously the Browns had been members of the Cross View Church, and Susan had spent a happy six years there as a member of a circle composed largely of mothers in their thirties. When Sam's career forced them to leave that congregation, Susan's interests changed to adult Christian education and that was the focus of most of her volunteer work in the churches they had joined in succeeding years including Trinity. In most of these congregations the women's organizations were composed of older women who were not employed outside the home. Susan's work as an office manager kept her from attending daytime activities at the church, such as the women's fellowship.

Shortly after joining Trinity Church Susan had met Gertie Baxter and soon they discovered that the nine years' difference in age was offset by much they had in common, and they became friends. Gertie who had been widowed when she was forty-seven, turned out to be one of Susan's most supportive, understanding, and warmest friends during those long months that followed Sam's sudden death. The companionship with this younger widowed woman also helped Susan gradually come to accept the fact that she also was a widow. Up until Sam's death Susan's stereotype of a widow was of an old, infirm, and dependent woman, a stereotype confirmed by those thrice-weekly visits to Sam's mother after they had moved here. The combination of the shock of Sam's sudden

death, living in an empty house, beholding an aging widow
when she looked in the mirror, sleeping alone in that big bed,
eating alone, and going alone to visit her mother-in-law in the
nursing home required a difficult period of adjustment for
this energetic woman. Gertie Baxter was of immense help as
those months slowly passed. Susan had been deeply in love
with her husband and she resented the fact that they had only
four years together following his "divorce" from that mistress
called "the company." In many ways those were the happiest
four years of their marriage. Unlike Gertie, who suggested
that the sequence was bereavement followed by independence followed by a sense of liberation, Susan did not feel
liberated. She felt forsaken, lonely, isolated, bitter, abandoned, deserted, and rejected. It was not until six years
following Sam's death that Susan began to understand
Gertie's reference to liberation.

Eventually she agreed to accompany Gertie to that circle,
which was composed largely of widowed women—a sharp
contrast to the circle Susan had been in a number of decades
earlier at Cross View Church. During those eighteen months
Susan missed only two meetings of that circle, both to go and
greet the arrival of a new grandchild, but she had displayed a
low level of visibility in the Women's Fellowship. In fact, she
had attended only three of those ten-times-a-year general
meetings when she appeared that April to be introduced by
Gertie as the new nominee for the office of president. This
was one reason why her nomination was not greeted by
thunderous applause. Many of the women at that meeting
felt they barely knew Susan. A couple did not even recognize
her. Several had been hoping the nominating committee
would be able to find a "dynamic young woman" and were
disappointed when "another old widow" was nominated.

While unsure of her role in this new office, which she had
accepted largely as a way to repay Gertie for her beautiful
friendship, Susan reflected on her life and concluded (a) God
had been good to her, (b) life had been good to her, (c) she
had four loving and supportive children with four supportive
spouses and eleven grandchildren, (d) given a choice between
the sudden and completely unexpected death of a husband

or watching a spouse go through many months of a painful terminal illness, she and Sam may have been lucky after all, (e) Trinity Church had been good to her, (f) this circle that Gertie headed had become a caring and treasured mutual support group, (g) she and Sam had forty-three wonderful years together and she should be thankful for that, (h) she was grateful for her excellent health and abundant energy, and (i) the future could be both challenging and fun.

Trinity Church had been founded in 1903, reached a peak in size in 1927, experienced twenty years of numerical decline, began to reach a new generation of younger families in the years after World War II and set new records in both worship and Sunday school attendance which required an expansion of the physical facilities, watched those numbers decline in the 1960s, considered closing during the second of two successive mismatches between pastor and parishioners, welcomed a new and energetic minister, Greg Sanders, in 1986, and was once again growing in numbers, morale, and enthusiasm as it programmed to reach the "baby boomers."

The Women's Fellowship (formerly simply "the Guild") peaked in numbers, enthusiasm, activities, and support for missions during the mid-1950s. As the years rolled by, it had gradually grown older and smaller (shrinking from eleven circles in 1957 to the current four), but the line on the graph showed a slow gradual decline that did not reflect the ups and downs of the congregation as a whole for those recent decades. The Women's Fellowship had survived (1) the shrinking in the size of Trinity Church, (2) one treasurer who could not account fully for all receipts or expenditures, (3) one minister who was determined to dissolve it as an obsolete and irrelevant remnant from yesteryear, but who left Trinity after a twenty-nine-month pastorate before he could do excessive damage, (4) the gradual evolution in the national emphasis of the women's organization of that denomination from missions to social action, (5) the recommendation that every circle be constituted with a new membership annually, (6) two different denominationally initiated names for the women's organization, and (7) a series of recommendations in changing the organizational structure and nomenclature of the local units.

That, briefly, is the scene Susan Brown inherited as she succeeded May Woodward as the president of the Women's Fellowship of Trinity Church.

When Gertie approached her about becoming the new president, Susan's first eleven responses were, "No, thanks," "I'm flattered, but no thanks," "I'm not the one you want for that job," "No," "No, thanks," "No," "NO," "No," "NO!" "NO!" and "ABSOLUTELY NOT!"

When she accepted, with great reluctance, Gertie's continued pleas to take the job, Susan included three conditions: (1) Gertie would continue on the executive committee, (2) May Woodward and Harriet O'Brien also would continue to serve on the executive committee, and (3) the other four would be replaced and two of the three other new members must be women born after 1945. The nominating committee happily agreed to those conditions.

When Harriet O'Brien heard Susan wanted her to continue, she stopped Susan in the corridor after worship one Sunday morning and said, "If you want me to continue on the executive committee, I'll be glad to do that, but you should know in advance I'm not the one to support the status quo. I want to see the Fellowship revitalized but so far I've not found much support. If you want to make some changes, I'm with you, but if you are content to keep things going as they have been, I'm not the one you want."

"I had a hunch that's the way you felt," replied Susan, "and that's why I wanted you to stay on the executive committee. I'll need some allies, and Gertie tells me you would be a good one."

The Women's Fellowship at Trinity Church had always operated on a July-1-to-June-30 year so Susan took office several weeks after her election in April. She called the first meeting of the executive committee for the second week in July. The new committee consisted of Susan, immediate past president May Woodward, Gertie Baxter, Harriet O'Brien, and three new members. One was the fifty-two-year-old Mary Rizzo. Mary's fiance had been killed in Vietnam many years earlier and Mary had never married. She lived alone and worked as a secretary for a cousin who had his own small insurance office. Mary was in her ninth year on the missions committee at Trinity Church and had been a member of the Fellowship for nearly twenty years, but this was her first term on the executive committee.

A second newcomer was Jennifer Jefferson, a mother of two who had been forced to go back to work as a nurse three years earlier when her husband had walked out on her to live with his twenty-three-year-old secretary. Jennifer was still struggling over whether she should divorce him or pray for a reconciliation.

The third was Lisa Winfield who had graduated from law school at twenty-three, married at twenty-nine, and had become the first female partner in the second largest law firm in the city at thirty-one. Two years later she took a two-month leave of absence to give birth to a daughter and returned to work while her mother-in-law cared for the baby during the day. At age thirty-five she was fully conscious of the fact that the biological clock was running and was delighted to discover she was pregnant once again. Six weeks after her son was born, she went back to the office on schedule. On her third day back at work, she asked her partners for a two-year leave of absence. When they laughed and told her she should have chosen the "Mommy track,"[3] rather than the partnership track, she went home angry and depressed. As she cuddled her adorable son that evening, she made her decision, told her husband the news, and began to make notes on a yellow legal pad. The next morning she met with three of the senior partners and announced, "This firm has been good for me, and I've been good for this law firm. Therefore I feel I owe you a choice. What's your preference? Grant me a two-year leave of absence? Offer me an equitable financial settlement to resign from the partnership? Or go to court and read about the case in the newspapers?"

"That's a rather limited range of options," replied the most militant of the three men. "Why don't you simply resign, leave on good terms, and when you're ready to come back, we'll give you consideration for whatever opening we have at that time?"

"Because I'm not a secretary here," replied Lisa. "I'm a partner. As you know, there's a world of difference between those two roles in a law firm. I'm in no hurry. I can wait until four o'clock, but I need a decision today."

"You know we can't work it out that quickly," angrily replied one of the senior partners.

"OK, make it five o'clock," cheerfully replied Lisa. "You guys are used to giving other people deadlines, so you should know how to meet one."

A few minutes after four o'clock, a fourth senior partner, who had been in court that morning, and who was a good personal friend of Lisa's, came into her office and offered her what he described as "a generous settlement" to resign her partnership.

Lisa replied, "That's not quite half of what I would consider a fair settlement." The senior partner walked out without a word.

Thirty minutes later this senior partner returned with an improved offer. After twenty minutes the two of them agreed to split the difference, shook hands, and sat down to write the memorandum of agreement. By the time they finished, everyone else had left, and the senior partner said to Lisa, "I still don't understand why you want to give all of this up. You and I both know you have the best legal mind in this firm."

"I'll explain that Tuesday when I come by to sign the papers," replied Lisa as she headed for the elevator.

As per agreement, at eleven o'clock the following Tuesday morning Lisa returned to sign the papers terminating her relationship with that law firm. Only two of the partners appeared for this brief meeting in the conference room. As he handed her a check, the senior partner who had negotiated the agreement said, "You promised you would explain to me why you're willing to give this up. What's your reason?"

"It's a matter of comparisons. Picture in your mind's eye your remaining partners, the impressive law library down the hall, my office, and the rest of the staff. Now look at Jacob Nathaniel here," explained Lisa as she happily and proudly looked at her seven-week-old son whom she was holding in her arms. "Who would give you up for all of that? Not me! Now, let's go, Jake, and clean out Mommy's office."

Most of the rest of the staff spent the next ninety minutes taking turns holding Jacob, telling Lisa how much they would miss her, envying her intestinal fortitude, wondering aloud how she could walk away from all of this to be a homemaker, helping her pack, wishing her well, pleading with her to be sure to come back and see them, expressing resentment over the firm's refusal to give her a leave of absence, silently wishing Lisa would tell them the amount of that check, and largely keeping to themselves the jealousy they felt for Lisa's sense of venturesomeness and independence.

Two weeks later Lisa's mother-in-law called and said, "Thursday afternoon is the monthly meeting of my circle. Why don't you come with me? We meet at the church at eleven, and they provide child care, but I need to call in today if you want to come, to be sure the woman in charge of the nursery will be prepared for a two-year-old and a baby."

"I don't think so," replied Lisa, as she imagined a gathering of a dozen women from her mother-in-law's generation meeting for three hours.

"Come on, give us a chance," pleaded her mother-in-law. "If you decide this isn't for you, I won't ever bother you again. There'll be at least three women your age there."

"Okay," conceded Lisa, more out of a sense of obligation than a desire to go. "When will you pick me up?"

That Thursday was the first time Lisa met Jennifer Jefferson and two other young mothers. Jennifer, who was a nurse at the hospital on the three-to-eleven evening shift, was there with her mother. Vicki Javier also was accompanied by her mother while Kristin Hassey came with her mother-in-law.

A couple of years earlier Dorothy Beeman, one of the longtime members of the Ruth Circle, had suggested, "We ought to take our name more seriously and become an intergenerational circle. As you all know, our daughter, Kathy, is divorced and has come home to live with us, but there's no circle for women her age. Charlotte, your daughter is back living with you. Helen, your daughter, Vicki, lives only a few blocks down the street from you, and she is home all day with her kids. Why don't we invite all three to come to our next meeting?"

The following month all three of these younger women showed up at circle meeting and discovered they had a lot in common. The next month, Jennifer Jefferson came with her mother, who had the responsibility for the devotional message, and used Ruth 1:15-18 as her text. Thus began the transformation of the Ruth Circle into an intergenerational group.

By the time Lisa appeared for the first time, Kathy Beeman had remarried and moved to Houston but Jennifer Jefferson, Vicki Javier, and Kristin Hassey were devoted members of the Ruth Circle as were two other younger mothers, but they were less regular in their attendance.

In understanding what happened next in the Women's Fellowship at Trinity Church, it is essential that this role of the Ruth Circle as an entry point for a new generation of women be given its just recognition.

Several years later, as she reflected on her role in Trinity Church, Lisa declared, "The existence of this circle and my mother-in-law's invitation to come to that meeting have turned out to be at least as big a turning point in my life journey as my earlier decision to go to law school. The Ruth Circle is where I met Jennifer and Vicki, who today are my closest friends. I had learned to meet and make friends at the office, at bar association meetings, while playing tennis with my husband, and on other occasions. But as a mother of two children, who suddenly one day dropped out of the practice of law, I needed some new friends who shared my new interests. Jennifer and Vicki not only are about my age, but they also have some of the same faith questions about their spiritual journey and about value systems that I have. In addition, the Ruth Circle also has opened up doors for me to other points where I can participate in the life and ministry of Trinity Church."

That is part of the background that led Lisa Winfield to be present at that July meeting of the executive committee chaired by Susan Brown.

—FRIAR TUCK

Deciding to revitalize
the Women's Fellowship
rather than re-create yesterday
is the most vital of decisions!

After opening the meeting with a brief devotional message and a prayer for God's guidance in their deliberations, Susan said, "We have two years together to begin the process of building a new future for this Women's Fellowship. What do each one of you want to see happen during these next years to make this a stronger and more vital organization? What's your number-one wish?"

"I already told you mine when we talked about your becoming the new president," began Gertrude Baxter. "I think we ought to have a bazaar every year. We give a lot of people a chance to be involved, we get better acquainted with one another, and we raise a chunk of money for missions. Back in February I was the only one to dissent when the decision was made to abandon the bazaar."

"But that was the recommendation of the majority," responded May Woodward somewhat defensively. "A lot of our women are getting too old to do all of that work."

"Hold it," interrupted Susan. "We'll discuss these later. At this time all we're going to do is build a list of what you all want to see happen in the next two years."

"I would like to see us get back to a greater emphasis on missions," declared Mary Rizzo. "That's our central purpose, and we've been doing less and less each year to support missions. That's my wish, more emphasis on missions."

"We need to reach more younger women," wished May Woodward. "I think we've made a start by getting Jennifer, Lisa, and Mary to serve on the executive committee, but I wish we could attract an even larger number of women in their twenties and thirties."

"My wish overlaps May's," explained Lisa Winfield. "I also would like to see more younger women, and I think one way of doing that would be to strengthen the intergenerational aspects of the Fellowship. Our circle is the only one that draws a lot of people from two different generations, but I wish we could do more of that. Maybe I'm unusual and I know I'm lucky, but my mother-in-law is one of my closest personal friends."

"You are unusual and you are lucky," interrupted Harriet O'Brien. "I have one daughter and two daughters-in-law and none of them would be caught dead in our Women's Fellowship! Fortunately none of them live around here, so we get along pretty well."

"You are lucky and you have a wonderful mother-in-law, Lisa," offered May Woodward. "She's been a good friend of mine for years, and I know she thinks the world of you, but there's an old saying that covers a lot of people: Every generation has two sets of enemies, their parents and their children."

"My wish is that we could reach out to more mothers who have to work and have children to care for," urged Jennifer Jefferson in an effort to get the meeting back on track. "As you all know, I'm separated from my husband and I know there are a lot of other women out there in similar circumstances, but we're not reaching them."

"My wish overlaps what you've all said," declared the blunt, outspoken Harriet O'Brien, "but takes a different form. I wish we could start two new circles in each of the next two years. You go over to that new shopping mall on Tuesday afternoon and you can see women of all ages going into those new stores. I think we need some new circles to be able to compete. Now, Susan, what's your wish?"

"As I told you before, Harriet, when I agreed to take this job I did it because I'm convinced the time has come either to revitalize the Women's Fellowship or else fold it up and replace it with a new organization. I'm ready to devote the next two years of my life to helping make that happen. So, I have several wishes. One is to turn those monthly general meetings into events people will want to attend and when they go home, they'll feel glad they made the effort to come. A second is to drop the median age of our membership by at least twenty years. A third is to double the membership in two years. A fourth is to become more responsive to the needs of women that aren't being met by any other organization or group here at Trinity, and a fifth is to introduce a new generation of leaders into the Women's Fellowship."

"That's a big job you've cut out for yourself," observed Mary Rizzo.

"Not for me, for all seven of us," corrected Susan.

"Well, one beginning point would be to organize a new arts and crafts circle to put on a bazaar this fall," declared Gertie Baxter, "and I'm willing to help organize a new circle to do that."

"Oh, we can't do that," protested May Woodward. "Don't you remember back in April at the general meeting there was an overwhelming majority in support of the recommendation to cancel the bazaar? Besides, we will need the permission of the general meeting to organize a new circle, and the next general meeting isn't until September."

"May, you have to remember our group is a voluntary association of women and no one is legally required to belong to it," explained Lisa Agnes Winfield. (One reason Lisa kept her middle name, rather than replacing it with her own surname when she married Jack Winfield was she liked that new set of initials, L.A.W.) While in law school Lisa had been intellectually stimulated and greatly influenced by the writings of Lon Fuller. "One way to wreck a voluntary association is to focus on telling people what they cannot do. The way to build a strong and vigorous voluntary association is to challenge people to do what they know is beyond their capabilities. Every great choir director or symphony conductor or football coach knows that. Susan's role as president of a voluntary association is to challenge all of us to do more than we believe we can do, and our job as an executive committee is to support and to help her."

"I have to agree with Mary," reflected Harriet. "Susan's got some big plans, but I'll do everything I can to help turn them into reality. I have a lot more time than money, so, Susan, tell me what you want me to do and let's get started! If a bazaar is the place to begin, I'll be glad to help Gertie get it organized."

Nineteen months later Susan came to the reluctant conclusion that Mary Rizzo had been right. She had carved out a far bigger and more complex agenda than could be accomplished in two years.

One January morning she stopped in to have a cup of coffee with her loyal ally, Gertrude Baxter. A half hour later Susan floated her final balloon. "Gertie, what do you think of my offering to take a second two-year hitch as president of the Women's Fellowship?"

Gertrude blinked, paused for a few seconds, and replied, "Well, as far as I can recall, no one's ever served two *consecutive* terms before, but I don't believe there's any law against it. In fact, as I think about it, I believe nearly everyone would be delighted if you would." (A year later one of the members in a nursing home recalled for the edification of a niece that several decades earlier May Woodward's mother had served for seven consecutive years as the president of the Guild and before her Vera Heath's mother had held that office for eight consecutive years. "Of course, in those days," added this frail, ninety-six-year-old woman with a crystal clear memory, "that was the only place, other than the Sunday school, where a woman could be a leader or teacher in the church. The men ran practically everything. It's better today, don't you think?" asked this lady of her sixty-seven year-old visitor.)

By the end of her second two-year term, vigorous and energetic Susan Brown could point to a Women's Fellowship that included 273 women in sixteen circles. The median age of this membership was 43 years—meaning one-half had passed their forty-third birthday and one-half had not yet reached that age. More than two hundred women had joined in these four years.

One of the changes that evoked the most comments and compliments was the growth in the attendance at those monthly general meetings. For years most of these monthly gatherings had drawn 30 to 45 participants, at least half of whom came out of a sense of obligation rather than anticipation of a meaningful experience. Now the attendance ranged between 85 and 110 and twice had passed 150, but that is a story for a subsequent chapter.

When she began her fourth year as president, her pastor, Greg Sanders, who had been a creative and helpful ally, suggested, "Susan, I think this experience has prepared you to leave us and go out where our denomination needs to start a new mission and do that. With this practice behind you, I expect you could build a 500-member church in four or five years or less."

While he was attempting to combine a compliment and a joke in one paragraph, that pastor was offering an excellent analogy. Susan had utilized many of the techniques and procedures that often are used in organizing a fast-growing new mission. Among these were (1) organizing new groups in response to the needs of people rather than expecting the agenda of the Women's Fellowship to attract large numbers of new people, (2) utilizing the gifts, skills, time, talents, and energy of allies and coalitions rather than attempting to do everything by herself, (3) accepting a creative, persistent, and patient, but aggressive initiating leadership role for herself, (4) planning and managing large group events using large group dynamics, (5) placing less reliance on invitations and more emphasis on commitments in asking people to join in a new venture, (6) affirming, supporting, thanking, and challenging all of her volunteer allies, (7) celebrating every success, (8) recognizing the need for and the value of a highly redundant system of internal communication as the organization grew in size and complexity, (9) seeking to implement a vision of a new tomorrow rather than attempting to do yesterday over again, and (10) continuing to be sensitive to the needs of her allies and co-workers.

An example of this last characteristic came when the thirty-eight-year-old Jennifer Jefferson discovered one day that after six years of separation, her husband had (a) walked out on the girl friend he had moved in with earlier, (b) moved in with a sexy young chick who insisted she wanted to become his wife, and (c) notified Jennifer that he was initiating divorce proceedings. This was a shock to the forgiving

th, Susan had been
ed, but had not re-
d. This gave her
concentrate on the
n's Fellowship rath-
focus on relating to
husband. Occasion-
eg kidded her that
ad married the
n's Fellowship.

h, Susan's twelve
s an office manager
ed her with excel-
dership and organi-
l skills including a
ness to delegate *both*
ty and responsibili-
also had learned
o plan and lead
g sessions.

ose moves from one
n far above average
os with strangers, in
nflicts.

asset. She fell com-
older adult leader."
liberated from the
tion and a detailed
She displayed zero
n's organization of
morrow, not yester-

own received both
sm. The decision to
was the pet project
rand new member,
e the annual bazaar
dit for salvaging it

Jennifer, who had been reared in the Catholic Church, did not believe in divorce, had left the Catholic Church to join a Protestant congregation when she had married this man eighteen years (one-half of her lifetime) earlier, and was still praying for the miracle of a reconciliation with this man she still loved.

Shortly after she heard the news, Susan called Harriet O'Brien who responded, "Let's get some rope and go hang that skunk!" Susan's next three

calls were to Kristin Hassey, who already knew the story, to Vicki Javier, and to Lisa Winfield. The four of them immediately formed a mutual support group for Jennifer that included Lisa handling all the legal work. Out of this eventually came a new circle for hurting women. (This and other circles will be described in more detail in chapter 5.)

Before examining in more detail this transformation of the Women's Fellowship at Trinity Church, it must be noted that Susan Brown and her allies were working in a favorable setting that made it easy to accomplish these changes in only four years. Susan had at least a dozen factors going for her.

One of these was the numerical decline of the Women's Fellowship for nearly four decades. While this was both a cause and a product of a substantial degree of passivity, that passivity also meant that Susan encountered little active opposition.

Second, Susan was, comparatively speaking, a newcomer. She had not spent thirty years learning what could not be done.

Third, she had enlisted some valuable allies with out-

Getting along with others is a trait to treasure!

—FRIAR TUCK

working leaders in the Women's Fello

Fifth, under the leadership of th
Sanders, the worship attendance-to-
Trinity had climbed substantially. Man
that change is relatively easy to introdu
when the worship attendance-to-mer
proving, but far more difficult when th

Sixth, the pastor, Greg Sanders, wa
was the third pastorate for Greg aft
program staff member in two much l
Greg was comfortable working in a
church and knew the value of progr
generation of younger adults, he enth
Susan's efforts.

Those fourteen years on the sta
churches also had taught Greg the val
that made it easy for him to affirm th
women's organization. Instead of beir
loyalty center, Greg knew this was g
essential to the future of Trinity Ch

BEING A LEADER CAN BE A BIT "TEETER-TOTTEROUS"!

A balanced leader can handle undue blame and credit for her actions!

—FRIAR TUCK

Eig
widow
marri
time t
Wome
er tha
a new
ally G
she h
Wome

Nin
years a
provid
lent lea
zationa
willing
author
ty. Sh
how t

meetings and the value of staff trainin

Tenth, as was pointed out earlier, all th
state to another had provided Susan wit
skills in meeting and building relationshi
adapting to change, and in resolving co

Eleventh, her age was a tremendous
fortably into the role of "the respected

Finally, like all leaders who have been
past, Susan had a strong future orienta
vision of what she wanted to see happen.
interest in trying to recreate the wome
1951. She lived in and for today and to
day.

Like most effective leaders, Susan B
undeserved credit and undeserved critic
plan another bazaar, for example, really
of Gertie Baxter, Harriet O'Brien, and a
Edna Pritchett, but those who hated to se
terminated gave Susan much of the cre

while those who wanted it scrapped criticized Susan for reversing the decision of that general meeting of the previous April.

What really happened was that two days after that executive committee meeting held in July, Susan met with Gertie and Harriet and said, "You two should know I have zero interest in the bazaar. I've only gone to two or three in all of my years in the church, and I hate to be made to feel guilty about not making something to be sold there. However, if you two think it's a good idea and that it would help revitalize this outfit, I say, go to it! Find some women to help you and tell me what you want me to do. Just don't ask me to make something to be sold there."

Likewise Susan received considerable criticism for scrapping the "fruit basket upset" system that called for women to move from one circle to another every year or two. What really happened was that Lisa Winfield, in her crusade to expand freedom of choice, had proposed a new system, which was adopted.

This new approach called for the following message to be delivered to each circle every spring: "One of our goals is to maintain the strength, continuity, and distinctive identity of each circle. Therefore, we are asking 40 percent of the women in each circle to sign up for another year. This will help maintain the continuity, identity, and traditions of that circle. We also want to encourage the cross fertilization of ideas and give our members the opportunity to meet and make new friends. Therefore, we are asking 30 percent of the women in each circle to volunteer either to move to another circle for this coming year or to sign up to help pioneer a new circle. The remaining 30 percent are free to move or stay."

This created a win-win set of alternatives and eliminated considerable nonproductive guilt. Those women who wanted to remain in the same circle with their friends could feel they were making a positive contribution by volunteering to help fill that quota. Those who wanted out could accept the role of a heroic volunteer, rather than fear they were being perceived as ungrateful traitors, by helping meet that goal of 30

RULES DON'T MAKE RELATIONSHIPS!

—FRIAR TUCK

Circles need an option on whether or not to circulate!

percent who would move on to another circle. Finally, this system (a) increased the number of women volunteering to help pioneer a new circle and (b) created a need for the existing circles to actively recruit replacements for those who left.

Despite Susan's repeated efforts to give credit where it was due, those who thought it unnecessary and excessively complicated blamed her while those who saw it as a stroke of genius gave Susan the credit that should have gone to Lisa, but neither worried about that.

Frequently a new agenda must be introduced if the goal is to revitalize any large established and tradition-oriented organization. That often requires new leadership, but that requires another chapter.

CHAPTER THREE

The Importance of Leadership

At the top of the list of ways to revitalize any organization, whether it be a political party, a congregation, a baseball team, a tired business that is losing money and customers, a small private college, a high school, or a service club, is new, creative, goal-oriented, skilled, enthusiastic, inspirational, persistent, aggressive, imaginative, and challenging leadership. The women's organization in American Protestantism is not an exception to that generalization.

Eight ways to kill your favorite group!
—FRIAR TUCK

Susan Brown's experience at Trinity Church is offered to illustrate that point. Several facets of that experience can be used to illustrate the impact of her leadership.

Counterproductive Recommendations

The first is to compare the recommendations for the coming year that came out of the executive committee during May Woodward's last year as president with the agenda that

How to add,
even while subtracting!
— FRIAR TUCK

Susan and her allies prepared. The recommendation that May's group prepared included eight of the essential ingredients that have been widely used, often with great success, to undermine the health, vitality, and future of a women's fellowship. First, the decision to merge the Esther and Martha circles is a common feature of the cutback syndrome. Merging two dying circles is not automatically a bad idea, but it should never be the first recommendation in a new action plan, and it should never stand alone. If it is decided to recommend the merger of two circles (or two Sunday school classes or two choirs or two youth groups), that proposal should be a minor component of a larger approach. This might be stated as, "In order to reach women who are not now involved in our Women's Fellowship, we propose to organize two new circles during the coming year, one for this group of women and a second circle in response to that need. Incidentally, we also are recommending the merger of the Esther and Martha circles, which means we will have a net gain of only one circle." At a minimum every proposed merger of two groups should be accompanied by plans for the creation of at least one new circle.

In other words, when retrenchment appears to be an appropriate step, the primary focus should not be on cuts, but rather on new opportunities. The best leaders seek to provide more than was promised even when cutbacks in one part of the organization may appear to be necessary. The best leaders are repelled by the cutback syndrome and are attracted by challenges that blend risk and innovation.

Another counterproductive recommendation was the suggestion to play "fruit basket upset" every year, instead of every other year. In an organization (a) built heavily on friendship ties and interpersonal relationships and (b) composed largely of mature adults, this often turns out to be an effective means of reducing the numbers. This rule often sounds at-

BOY! WE'RE NOT LOSIN', WE ARE CREATING AN HISTORICAL LANDMARK IN THE MIDDLE of NOWHERE!

WOW!

Good leaders can create challenges out of cutbacks!
—FRIAR TUCK

tractive to the forty-seven-year-old who enjoys meeting and making new friends. Many mature adults, however, have experienced an erosion of that skill. They want to maintain existing friendships, not be coerced into making new ones. When the choice is between staying home or going to a circle meeting that will be a gathering of longtime friends, it is relatively easy to make the effort to get up and go. When, however, that choice is between staying home and going to a meeting that may consist of one or two close friends, two or three acquaintances, and a half dozen strangers, it is easy to conclude, "I think I'll stay home today and invite Violet and Hazel to come over here some afternoon next week."

When the train stops to pick up new passengers, it is easy for a few who have been riding it for many miles to slip off unnoticed.

Although persuasive arguments can be mustered against money-raising activities in the church, a third counterproductive recommendation was to cancel the bazaar. As will be explained in more detail in chapter 5, the bazaar can be an

WHEN IT COMES TO MEETING STRANGERS, TEDDY AND I WOULD JUST AS SOON STAY HOME!

—FRIAR TUCK

Circles remain successful when their participants remain basically familiar!

attractive entry point for newcomers. The decision to eliminate the bazaar could have been defended if it had been accompanied by a recommendation to create two or three equally inviting new entry points for potential future members. That was not done.

While adopting missions in Africa as a study theme was commendable, it was somewhat presumptuous to expect that all the women in every one of those four circles would find this to be a top priority concern. As Lisa Winfield pointed out later, the Women's Fellowship at Trinity Church (unlike the Women's Missionary Societies of the nineteenth century) really had evolved into a voluntary association. It no longer was the "high demand" organization or cause it had been decades earlier. One alternative would have been to transform it back into a high demand missionary society (as the WMU is today in some Southern Baptist congregations). A second alternative, which Susan Brown subsequently introduced, would be to assume that (a) Trinity Church resembled a voluntary organization rather than a high demand congregation, (b) over the previous decades many people had joined Trinity Church for a wide variety of reasons, (c) the religious needs of some of the members today are not the same as they were when those people originally joined Trinity Church, (d) each new pastor attracts a new and different strata of members, and (e) given that setting, it may be necessary to offer people choices if any one organization seeks to be responsive to that huge variety of religious needs that people bring to that church.

In addition, as was pointed out in chapter 1, study tends to be an exclusionary, not an inclusionary, organizing principle.

A fifth recommendation that came out of May Woodward's executive committee that merits careful evaluation was the proposal for those neighboring congregations to cosponsor three bus trips for senior citizens. If this was understood to be a community service project, it should be commended. If it was intended to be a means of identifying and attracting new members for the Women's Fellowship at Trinity Church, it should be challenged. The basis for that challenge is "intercongregational cooperation in programming and numerical growth tend to be mutually exclusive goals." Thousands of congregations have demonstrated the validity of that generalization. If this was intended to be an opportunity for potential new members to become acquainted with the Women's Fellowship at Trinity Church, a unilateral approach probably would be more productive.

Instead of canceling the

Rotating our members has taken away our openness!
—FRIAR TUCK

I CAN'T UNDERSTAND WHY WE DON'T HAVE MORE FOLKS INTERESTED IN OUR EXCITING STUDY OF MADAGASCAR?

AFRICA STUDY TODAY

Study groups tend to be exclusionary!
—FRIAR TUCK

We all tend to pass up passive proposals!

— FRIAR TUCK •

tradition of the annual mother-daughter banquet because of poor attendance, it might have been more productive to have examined why the attendance had dropped. This may have been a timely recommendation, but again it would have been better if accompanied by a recommendation to replace the mother-daughter banquet with a new and more attractive annual event. This appears to to be the cutback syndrome at work.

The recommendation to prepare a set of posters to publicize the Women's Fellowship and to invite others to join it has several deficiencies. It is a passive gesture. Nothing was said about activities that would attract women to join. A better proposal would have been to focus first on, "What will we do?" and second on, "How do we invite more women to join us in doing this?" This was a cart-before-the-horse recommendation. The walkathon described in chapter 4 could be the theme for a series of posters. That would be an invitation to join in an adventure that usually is far more attractive than an invitation to join an organization.

Finally, the recommendation to allocate the first two hundred dollars to purchase dishes, silverware, and pans (a) reinforced the image of a "housekeeping organization that takes care of the kitchen," (b) undercut the priority on missions, and (c) was unlikely to be perceived as a challenging and exciting goal by potential new members. It might have been wiser for that expenditure to have come out of the operating budget of Trinity Church or the trustees' account or memorial funds or a special offering or an adult Sunday school class' budget.

By contrast, the recommendations that came from Susan Brown's leadership reflected a greater emphasis on responding to the needs of people, on creating new circles for new members, on building a new tomorrow, on reaching and serving more people, and on attracting a new generation of members. (The details of Susan's program will be described in greater detail in succeeding pages.)

These critical comments are not offered to discredit May Woodward or her executive committee. That group of loyal ladies had inherited and was following in a tradition of passive decline, of responding to reduced numbers by adopting the cutback syndrome, and by affirming a secondary role as responsible for the kitchen.

The point to be lifted up from this review is to contrast two approaches to leadership. In one it is tempting to react to present circumstances by

WHO WOULD HAVE THOUGHT THAT STRETCHING IS A MEANS OF PERSONAL GROWTH!

Growing women's groups offer a variety of choices!
—FRIAR TUCK

SORRY, BUT I ALWAYS LEAVE MY APRON AT HOME!

Women's organizations have better challenges than housekeeping!
—FRIAR TUCK

ANY OF US CAN FIND A USEFUL ROLE BEHIND A STRONG LEADER! (GULP!)

Not all of us can be leaders, but we all need to be part of a winning organization!
—FRIAR TUCK

adopting what later can be seen as counterproductive recommendations.

A second approach is that of the initiating leader who sets out to build a new future. May's approach to leadership was to react to an agenda that was presented to her. Susan's style was to initiate and to build her own agenda.

Why Keep Her?

At this point someone may ask, "If May Woodward was so ineffective, why did Susan insist she continue on the executive committee?"

Susan, who after twelve years as the office manager of what had turned out to be a rapidly growing business, had a high degree of confidence in her own ability to evaluate people.

In Susan's eyes May was a loyal, hardworking, and dedicated follower who had been miscast as a leader when she became president of the Women's Fellowship. Susan concluded that May (a) needed the satisfaction and fulfillment of being part of a winning team before she became too old to serve, (b) had the qualities needed to be a valuable player on the team—she simply should not be expected to be the captain, (c) had earned the respect of all the longtime members and would be an effective legitimatizer of what would be happening, (d) enjoyed talking on the phone to her friends and Susan wanted accurate and positive statements fed into that grapevine, not negative rumors, and (e) loved the Lord and both wanted and needed a place on the executive committee as one means of serving her Lord.

Susan assumed that much of what she had in mind would not automatically win the enthusiastic endorsement of all the longtime members. May could help win the support of some and neutralize others. Susan expected Harriet O'Brien to intimidate into neutrality many of those May could not win over to the new agenda.

How Big Is Big?

Susan Brown had spent twenty-five years overseeing a household that included, at its peak years, six human beings, a succession of cats, and, for nine years, one collie. Subsequently she had spent twelve years managing an office, which at its peak had twenty-two people working under Susan's supervision. Her older son, David, had taught fourth grade in an elementary school for seventeen years and always complained when he had more than thirty children in a class. Susan's husband, Sam, had a superb tenor voice and always sang in the church choir wherever they lived. On only two or three Sundays out of the year did the choir at Trinity Church include more than thirty-five voices. When they came to Trinity Church, Sam and Susan had joined an adult Sunday school class that usually had between twenty-five and thirty-five in attendance. When she was elected president of the Women's Fellowship, Susan had ten grandchildren, and she almost always was able to call each one correctly by name.

The Women's Fellowship at Trinity Church carried 113 names on the membership roll, although many of them rarely or never attended a circle meeting. Susan may have been the only person in Trinity Church who believed this was a BIG organization. May Woodward, and all her predecessors for at least a quarter of a century, perceived the Women's Fellowship as a small organization that was growing older and smaller—most of these leaders appeared to act on the assumption the Women's Fellowship was simply "one big family."

Susan saw it as too large and too complex to even survive, much less to grow in numbers, without more structure. Her predecessors had operated on the assumption it was a small and shrinking organization that would thrive on informality and an ad hoc approach to the future. They followed a course

PLEASE BRING TO EACH MEETING THE NAMES AND ADDRESSES OF THOSE WHO COULD BE INTERESTED IN JOINING US!

Personal Evangelism: A way each of us can reach more of us!

— FRIAR TUCK

of action, unintentionally of course, to make that assumption into a self-fulfilling prophecy.

Consistent with her perspective Susan created a set of committees with clearly defined responsibilities and held them accountable. In addition she created a series of short-term task forces and coalitions to respond to specific needs.

One of the committees was assigned the responsibility of new member enlistment. Every circle was urged to ask every member to bring to every meeting the name and address of someone who might be interested in coming to the Women's Fellowship. These names were used as a resource in inviting women to help pioneer new circles, in seeking volunteers to work in the bazaar, and in that continuing effort to enlist new members.

Another new committee was assigned the responsibility of publishing a monthly newsletter that went to every member and every potential future member. The cost of printing and postage for this newsletter aroused some opposition on the grounds that this could be accomplished just as effectively and at a lower cost by including these announcements in Trinity's newsletter and in the Sunday morning bulletin.

Persistent Susan got her way, however, and offered several reasons for a separate newsletter for the Women's Fellowship. These included timing, a need to circulate it beyond the membership of Trinity Church in order to reach potential new members, the value of the newsletter in reinforcing the identity of the Women's Fellowship as a self-governing, self-financing, and self-propagating auxiliary, a recognition

of the fact that not everyone read the parish news-
letter, the value of redundant channels of commu-
nication, the appeal of a
single purpose newsletter
over a newsletter designed
for several audiences* and
as a means of encouraging
the creativity of the editors
and contributors.

Later on the methodical
Susan was appalled when
she discovered that circle
leaders were asked to serve
in that leadership role, but
were offered no training
or instructions and given
no specific help. Eventual-

Our own newsletter
can best open
the hearts of others
while enlarging our own!
—FRIAR TUCK

ly a committee was created to prepare a manual for circle
leaders and to offer two two-hour training sessions every year
for new circle leaders.

A task force, organized to identify the needs that could be
met by new circles, came in with a dozen suggestions.

May Woodward, like her predecessor, had relied largely on
the executive committee and the circles to provide most of the
structure needed for what in fact was a large organization.
This was supplemented by a few short-term committees such
as the nominating committee, the kitchen committee, and,
before they were canceled, the bazaar committee, and the
committee responsible for the annual mother-daughter banquet. Most of the administrative and planning responsibilities, however, were placed in the executive committee or
assigned to circle leaders.

---

*Many people read newsletters in the bathroom and that mundane fact of life should
influence the length of a newsletter.

By contrast, Susan Brown saw this as a big organization in need of more organizational structure if it was to grow in size, and she created the structure necessary to enable that to happen.

To a significant degree each of these two presidents created a self-fulfilling prophecy that was influenced by her assumptions about size, the weight of tradition, and what the future would bring.

Three Forks in the Road

Two years after Susan had completed her second term, some women in another church asked her, "What was the one critical factor that was the key variable in how and why that women's organization grew so fast in such a brief period of time?"

"I can't narrow it down to one," replied Susan. "There really were three critical decisions we made in the first months that were decisive. One was to redefine the boundaries for membership. Many years earlier, I discovered, someone in our denomination had coined the phrase, 'Every woman who is a member of this congregation is a member of the women's fellowship.' While this may have been well-intentioned, it was both nonsense and exclusionary. There was nothing in the vows of membership that required a new member to join any particular organization or group in that church. It might have worked with many of the women from my generation who were taught they should do what authority figures told them to do, but that won't work with the younger women of today. In addition, if you read it carefully, it suggests you have to be a member of this congregation to join the women's organization."

"What did you do to change that?" inquired a listener.

"We set a goal that at least one-fourth of the original members of any new circle would come from beyond the membership of Trinity Church. In a few cases a majority of the first members of a new circle were not members of the church. That was a key breakthrough, to define ourselves as an organization open to women who weren't members of Trinity Church.

"The second radical change was when we broadened the focus to a broader statement of purpose than simply missions. We never changed our bylaws, that would have been an unnecessary and diversionary battle, but we did run into some opposition. We offered them the choice," continued Susan, "of growing older and smaller or broadening the umbrella to include more younger women."

VISION CAN OVERCOME ENVIRONMENT!

Our dreams determine our direction and destination!
—FRIAR TUCK

"I'm not sure we could sell that back home," reflected one of the women. "Our denomination is very clear that we should concentrate our efforts on missions and only on missions."

"That brings us to what was our third big fork in the road," explained Susan, "but to understand this you'll need to know a little more about me. First, my husband and I both grew up in a Christian home. I learned about God and Jesus from the time I could begin to understand the English language. My husband's parents were more conservative theologically and far more strict than mine, and both of us went off to a Christian college when we finished high school. Neither of our parents would have taken the chance of sending us to a pagan state university even though that would have been cheaper. We had compulsory chapel every day as well as classes on the Bible, missions, and church history. Sam was two years ahead of me and we met and fell in love in college in what was clearly a Christian context.

"We both grew up in a world in which God, Jesus, going to Sunday school and to church were givens. Our parents

WOW! INSTEAD OF GROWING OLDER and SMALLER WE'RE GETTING BIGGER AND BETTER!

Women's Organizations grow when they focus on the religious needs of all their people!

FRIAR TUCK

instilled in us a strong loyalty to the church," continued Susan. "We had four children. Today one is a member of a spirit-filled charismatic congregation, one doesn't go to church at all, one is a member of a big independent fundamentalist church, and one is an active member of a church of our denomination. Watching the faith journey of our kids and their spouses taught me that not every person is at the same place on his or her faith journey as everyone else. No one church can meet the religious needs of every Christian. For some women the most important thing a women's organization can offer her is a chance to express her commitment to and support of missions. Missions, however, does not even make the list of urgent concerns of a lot of other women."

"But shouldn't those other needs be met by other organizations and groups in the church?" challenged someone else. "Does the women's organization have to be all things to all people? Why can't we just concentrate on missions and let someone else do the rest?"

"That's a critical fork in the road," responded Susan in her normal, methodical, precise, affirming, linear, and directive style. "First of all, do you want to limit yourself only to those women who place a high priority on missions? Second, why can't you have two or three or four themes? Third, the one thing I'm sure of is that the world out there is a lot more competitive than it was forty years ago. If we in our churches aren't responsive to all the religious needs of our people, they can easily find some other place that is. I would much rather encourage competition among the different organizations, classes, and programs in our church in meeting the needs of our people than to assign each one a narrowly defined purpose and watch people fall through the cracks.

"Now, let me get back to the question," continued Susan. "I said we faced three critical decisions that influenced our potential for growth. The first was to cast a bigger net and deliberately reach out to women beyond those who were members of Trinity Church. The second was to broaden our purpose beyond simply interest in and support of missions. The third was to aggressively start a lot of new groups in response to a variety of needs. Some of these did overlap what already was being done at our church, but our philosophy was to affirm redundancy rather than risk leaving needs unmet. We went from what originally was a missions organization that had evolved into a combination of fellowship, study, and missions to intentionally creating a broad umbrella under which we could respond to a lot of different needs."

"How did you make contact with all of these other women who weren't members of your church?" asked another woman.

"We took the initiative," replied Susan. "We advertised. We asked every member to be a recruiter, and we worked at it."

Should We Advertise?

One of the critical questions for every women's organization that is rarely asked is, Should we advertise? Most choose not to advertise and depend on members inviting other women or on newcomers coming in on their own initiative.

One of the few battles that the Reverend Greg Sanders consistently lost at Trinity Church was his plea for more money for publicity and advertising. Greg's goal was an amount equal to 5 percent of the operating budget for public relations. The closest he had come to a victory was one year an amount equal to 3 percent of the budget was initially approved, but that was cut by two-thirds when the finance committee had to reduce the proposed budget to match anticipated receipts.

SHE'S A WINNER OVER FEAR, FUZZINESS, AND FRUSTRATION!

Leadership ranks at the top of any list on how to revitalize your Women's Organization!

—FRIAR TUCK

At her third meeting of the executive committee Susan had won approval of her plan to send a letter to every member of the Women's Fellowship asking for a contribution of $5 up to $100 for a special fund to expand the membership. That letter was signed by all the women on the executive committee and produced $965. This paid the postage for mailing nearly 4,000 first-class letters over the next year, but that is part of the story in chapter 5.

The theme of this chapter is the potential impact of new, creative, competent, aggressive, enthusiastic, future-oriented, visionary, skilled, persistent, and goal-oriented initiating leadership. That ranks at the top of this list of 44 ways to revitalize the women's organization. In some, but not all congregations, the second best approach to revitalizing the women's fellowship may be to make the monthly general meeting a more attractive, meaningful, and enjoyable experience. For Susan Brown that also was a high priority.

CHAPTER FOUR

That Monthly General Meeting

A second useful approach to the revitalization of the women's fellowship in your church may be to transform those monthly general meetings from dull and perfunctory gatherings that rely largely on institutional loyalties to draw a crowd into attractive events that cause people to want to attend. This was one of Susan Brown's top priorities when she accepted the presidency of the Women's Fellowship at Trinity Church.

Susan had inherited a system that called for ten meetings annually. The three "big" ones were held in January, April, and September. The other seven were more routine gatherings. These seven smaller meetings were organized around a combination of fellowship, worship, a brief business session, a report on one mission project supported by that fellowship, an obligation to obey the denominational guidelines that call for monthly general meetings, refreshments, something to do if your day is largely empty, the introduction of new members, and habit. For the past forty years these seven meetings had been scheduled for two hours from 9:30 to 11:30 on the morning of the second Tuesday of every month. Sometime back in the 1960s it had been decided to drop the August meeting from the schedule because of vacations, and in the late 1970s, when Trinity Church was concentrating on cutting back on program in general under the leadership of an inept pastor, the July general meeting had been dropped from the schedule. In recent years attendance had fluctuated between seventeen and twenty-five at these meetings. Susan had attended only two of these before being elected president.

The three "big" general meetings were scheduled from ten

ABOUT THOSE MONTHLY MEETINGS...

We need to change its format if we wish to fulfill its potential!
—FRIAR TUCK•)

o'clock in the morning to two o'clock in the afternoon and included lunch, which helped increase the size of the crowd. These usually drew between thirty and forty-five women.

The April meeting was the annual business meeting and included adoption of the program for the coming year, the election of officers, a detailed financial report, and other institutional concerns.

The September luncheon always featured a missionary as the speaker and traditionally had been a "dress-up" occasion. May, Vera, and Evelyn could remember when nearly every woman attending the September luncheon came wearing a new hat or a new dress. The tables had been covered with linen tablecloths and adorned with fresh cut flowers. In recent years paper had replaced linen as the material for table coverings and napkins, and women in pant suits or slacks outnumbered those in hats and dresses. For many of the older women comfort had moved ahead of impressing others as the number-one criterion for selecting their dress for the September luncheon.

Traditionally, the theme for the January meeting had been a brief presentation by each circle of its special mission project for that year. As the number of circles grew smaller, this required less time so fellowship, food, and nostalgia became the unofficial theme of the January luncheon.

Susan created a special study committee consisting of Mary Rizzo, May Woodward, Vicki Javier, Kristin Hassey, and a relatively new member, the thirty-seven-year-old Barbara McGuire to propose recommendations for improving those general meetings. Kristin had been the secretary for the head of a small public relations firm before she dropped out of the labor force to rear a family. Before she married, Vicki had been on the administrative staff of the local community college that directed the night school program. Barbara McGuire was a creative, somewhat lonely, attractive divorced woman who lived alone and worked as a loan officer in a local bank.

THIS IS YOUR CHANCE TO SHINE! YOUR FRIENDS ARE HERE, YOU'RE ON PRIME-TIME, AND SOMEBODY UP THERE LIKES YOU!

Friendly competition between circles can make for the best of monthly meetings!
— FRIAR TUCK.

After a half dozen meetings this ad hoc group came up with a four-point set of recommendations.

First, in even numbered months the general meetings would be held in the evening and in odd numbered months they would be scheduled as daytime events. The obvious reason was to attract more women who worked outside the home during the day, but also to retain day meetings for those who worked evenings or on shifts.

Second, as the number of circles grew, each circle would be asked to accept responsibility for planning one meeting during the year. The exception, of course, was the April meeting which would continue to be the responsibility of the executive committee. For the first couple of years several circles had to accept the responsibility for two general meetings.

One reason for this recommendation was to reduce the work load on the executive committee. A second was to introduce a degree of competition. As was expected, on several occasions a circle would try to "outdo" the others in making their meeting a truly BIG event. A third reason was that this would guarantee at least the core of a crowd since most of the members of the circle responsible for the meeting

I'VE GOT TO GO TO CHURCH! ONLY I KNOW HOW to TURN ON the COFFEE MAKER AND FURNACE, and I HAVE the KEYS TO the REST ROOMS!

Giving folks
an assignment
assures their attendance!

—FRIAR TUCK.

could be expected to be present. A fourth reason was to enable those who were interested in doing so to enhance their skills in planning and running large group events. Finally, this would be a means of assimilating the new members of those new circles into the larger group.

Third, they recommended that every general meeting should have its own distinctive theme and that by the second year of this new approach those themes should be identified at least six months in advance to provide adequate time for publicity. A second reason for this requirement was to lengthen the time frame for planning so each circle would have sufficient time to plan an attractive event. Each circle would choose the theme it wanted for the meeting for which it was responsible. This, of course, also was a means of improving quality.

Fourth, Trinity Church should sponsor two training events during the next twelve months to teach people how to lead better large group meetings. This turned out to be the most valuable recommendation on the list.

A couple of months later the first of these was held under the leadership of a person who specialized in training people to plan and lead better large group meetings. Among the lessons learned that day the following two dozen points had a profound impact on the general meetings of the women's fellowship at Trinity Church.

1. Every meeting should have a distinctive purpose or theme and everyone invited to attend should have a statement of that purpose well in advance. This forced each circle to plan, to focus in more clearly on a specific theme, and to

articulate that theme well in advance in order to get out the publicity at least several months in advance.

IN THIS WAY, YOU'LL KNOW ME EVEN BEFORE YOU SEE ME!

FRIAR TUCK

—FRIAR TUCK

Name tags need to be readable at six feet!

2. Ask as many people as possible to accept a specific responsibility for that meeting. These responsibilities ranged from who would prepare that publicity sheet and the poster to who would preside to who would make sure one person at each table would be responsible for clearing away the dishes after refreshments or dessert to who would be in charge of the singing. The recommended ratio was that for every ten people expected to be present, at least six would have one clearly defined responsibility for which they had committed themselves well in advance.

3. The agenda to be circulated as part of that advance publicity should state clearly (a) the amount of time allocated for each item on the agenda and (b) the name(s) of the person(s) responsible for that item. One reason for this is to maintain the pace and keep the meeting from dragging. Another is to enable people to see in advance what are the important items on that agenda—these should be allocated the most time. A third is to publicize who will be involved. This is one means of increasing attendance. Some folks will make a special effort to come if they know in advance who will be present. A fourth is to minimize surprises. People should be forewarned about what will be discussed.

4. Name tags are important for those monthly general meetings and absolutely essential if the group is expecting women who have never attended a general meeting before. A useful approach is for each circle to design its own

distinctive name tag which will reinforce the identity of that circle. This is a means of reinforcing group cohesion in that circle as well as carrying the name of the wearer. The lettering should be sufficiently large that it can be read by the average seventy-year-old at a distance of six feet. In one congregation the women in one circle made their own T-shirts that bore the logo of that circle and carried the name of the wearer. (Not all women will endorse that plan!)

5. A subtle point made that Saturday was that every meeting includes both content and process. In planning it one person should be responsible for planning content and someone else should be responsible for the dynamics of the process.

Among other implications this means care should be exercised in selecting the person who will preside at that monthly general meeting. This does not have to be the circle leader. It does not have to be the person who is president of the women's organization in that church. It should be a person with skills in conducting a meeting, genuine sensitivity to others, someone with a sense of humor who can inject humor into the gathering when a change of pace is appropriate and someone who is comfortable before a large crowd. This is not the time to insist on "passing the job around so everyone has the chance to preside at a general meeting." Performance is far more important than egalitarianism in choosing that presiding officer.

6. If the discussion will cover controversial or divisive issues, build in a redundant system for surfacing dissenting views. One of the more effective means of discouraging people from coming back next month is to increase the chances they will leave without having what they perceive as a fair opportunity to express a dissenting point of view.

It may not be possible for the presiding officer to give everyone in the minority a chance to speak, but it is important that a range of dissenting views be articulated. This will enable the dissenter to leave reasonably satisfied. "Although I didn't get a chance to be heard, at least our position was stated, and I hope at least some of the people there know how we feel."

7. Operate on the assumption that everyone enjoys learning. Build into each meeting three or four opportunities for those present to learn what they will perceive as interesting or useful new knowledge. One way to entice people back to the next meeting is for them to leave saying to themselves, "I'm glad I came! I learned something new today."

8. Remember the walls can teach! It is not unusual for people to arrive early for that monthly general meeting. Therefore it can be useful to use the walls of the meting room to display posters, photographs, maps, letters from missionaries, and other items that describe the role and activities of the women's organization and affirm the distinctive identity of each circle.

9. Decide in advance whether the *primary* theme is information sharing or fellowship or problem solving or planning or therapy or a series of small discussion groups and make sure the seating arrangements are compatible with that theme.

10. The larger the number of people who are expected to be present, the more important are such factors as (a) acoustics, (b) lighting, (c) comfortable chairs, (d) rigid adherence to the schedule, (e) a wide choice of beverages when the time comes for refreshments, (f) a frequent change of pace, (g) name tags, and (h) a brief three-to-five-minute introductory orientation of why we are here.

11. One way to encourage people to return next month is for them to leave feeling, "I really had a good time!" Therefore build in humor, laughter, and opportunities for people to enjoy themselves.

12. Do not allocate any more time than the absolute minimum to hearing reports from standing committees. As a general practice all reports from standing committees and circles should be presented in printed form and the discussion should be limited. The larger the number of people in the room, the less time should be devoted to reports from standing committees.

The exception to this is reports from special ad hoc study committees or ad hoc action committees may deserve considerable time for presentation and discussion.

IT IS EASIER TO REVIVE THE LIVING THAN TO RESUSCITATE THE DEAD!

YE OLDE GENERAL MEETING TODAY

Devote more time to the birth of the new than trying to keep alive what is dying!

— FRIAR TUCK •

NOBODY GETS BY HER UNTIL THEY'RE A PART OF US!

I ♥ YA

Gregarious greeters minimize the chances of anyone going home feeling ignored!

— FRIAR TUCK •

13. Celebrate the formation of every new circle and the completion of every new special event or special accomplishment. Devote more time to the birth of the new and less time trying to keep alive that which is dying.

14. Whenever it is appropriate, lift up what was accomplished. Many people are more likely to return next month if they leave feeling, "Well, we got something done tonight." This may range from approving a budget to honoring a volunteer or retiring officer to resolving a long-festering dispute to celebrating a victory to electing officers to welcoming new members to a new learning experience. It often helps if the person presiding will take a few seconds to review what was accomplished at this meeting immediately before the benediction is pronounced. It may help to preface that summary with a reminder of the primary purpose of that particular gathering.

15. Make sure everyone in attendance is greeted correctly by name and wel-

comed by at least two other people. The most effective way of making sure this happens is to enlist three or four gregarious, cheerful, extroverted, and trained greeters for each monthly meeting. Minimize the chances that someone may go home thinking, "I don't know why I bothered to come. Nobody would have missed me if I had stayed home."

16. Stress the use of visual material. People remember more easily and more clearly what they see than what they hear. This may mean giving everyone a copy of the proposed budget, asking each circle to maintain an up-to-date membership roster on a poster than can be displayed at every general meeting, the use of color slides at that January meeting to recapture what happened during the past months, listing the names of all new members to be introduced at that meeting, the use of name tags, asking speakers to illustrate their lectures, and photographs of all new members on a poster.

17. If the attendance is expected to exceed forty participants, a piano or accordian or guitar or some other musical instrument should be available to accompany the singing. Men can sing a cappella, but women benefit from musical accompaniment. Music can be a powerful unifying force in a large group, it provides a change of pace, it can be an inspirational moment, and it gives everyone a chance to stand and stretch.

18. If at all possible, every monthly general meeting should include the announcement and celebration of a victory achieved by the women's organization. This may be a major accomplishment by one circle or the surpassing of a goal set for the entire fellowship, or an unanticipated success story or a victory by the regional or national women's organization of that denomination or perhaps something as simple as the purchase of new furniture for the church parlor or the birth of a baby to a missionary supported by that congregation or the formal reception of some new members.

It is important for people to leave feeling, "This organization is alive, things are happening, we're getting things done, and I'm proud to be part of it."

SHE GOT A REAL LIFT OUT OF COMING TODAY!

Every meeting can leave folks glad they came!

—FRIAR TUCK

YES, MADELEINE, I RECEIVED YOUR INVITATION LAST WEEK AND I'M GETTING ANOTHER MESSAGE RIGHT NOW!

Everyone needs three different kinds of invitations!

—FRIAR TUCK

19.   Every member should receive at least three invitations to attend in addition to the announcement in the newsletter. These can be postcards, telephone calls, face-to-face visits, a special mailing to every person who might attend, including potential new members or an announcement from the pulpit. The newsletter should be seen as only one of a redundant series of invitations.

20. This overlaps the last point, meetings should be designed to provide every member with a redundant set of reasons for attending. These may range from being with two or three close friends to having the opportunity to be heard on an important issue to sharing in the intercessory prayer for a friend in the hospital to shaking hands with Elvis Presley or the bishop to hearing an inspiring devotional message to fulfilling an obligation such as giving a report or serving as a greeter to the promise of a good meal to meeting a missionary being supported by that organization to learning

something new to having her own personal faith journey enriched to receiving affirmation.

21. At least once a year that monthly meeting should be designed to be a memorable experience. This can be done most effectively if it is held off the church property. A picnic in a public park or a dinner in someone's backyard is one possibility. A second is the annual retreat.

Once or twice a year the women's group in a West Coast church gathered in a hotel for a weekend retreat from Friday evening to Sunday afternoon. In October 1988 someone suggested that instead of traveling to the hotel by car the women should walk. This suggestion evolved into a twenty-mile-walkathon-public-witness fund-raiser-shared-experi-ence-memorable adventure. On the appointed day several score women gathered in response to this challenge, most of them proudly wearing T-shirts emblazoned with the slogan, "Walk His Way." Three generations of women shared in this adventure including several who had been born a half century or more before the founding of this fourteen-year-old congregation. What happened?

Friends, husbands, parents, children, and neighbors responded to the challenge to pledge money for each mile a person walked, and several thousand dollars was raised for a shelter for abused wives. The walkers paused now and then to chat with bystanders, to explain the cause they were advocating, to offer their witness to Christ, and to answer questions. One young bystander was so impressed she joined the walkathon.

Less visible, but equally significant, was the bonding that occurred among these women as they shared in this seven-hour walk. Old friendships were strengthened and reinforced. Acquaintances became close friends. Some people walk at a slower or faster pace than others and thus those who chose to walk at the same pace met and made new friends. Every six or seven miles the group stopped, gathered for a devotional time, and enjoyed refreshments or a meal. This also provided a chance to regroup and for members to choose new walking companions for the next few miles.

Despite centuries of being programmed to depend on

BUT...BUT... WHO WILL TELL THEM WHERE THE REST ROOMS ARE LOCATED!

Minimize
oral announcements !
—FRIAR TUCK

women to be the support groups, a number of men were able to function in a support role for these venturesome women as they drove ahead to scout the route, brought the food, and provided a choice of beverages to quench the thirst of the walkers.

Like any other memorable shared experience or adventure, the walkathon also provided a superb entry point for newcomers and facilitated the assimilation into the larger group of recent new members.

Could you make the next monthly general meeting of the women's fellowship in your church into a walkathon?

22. Minimize the number of oral announcements that must be made, make them early, and get them out of the way. One useful approach is to reproduce all the necessary announcements on paper and place a copy at each place at the table before the meeting begins. This reduces the time required for announcements, minimizes the chances of misleading communication, and gives the first arrivals something to read. This sheet of paper also may list the names of those who deserve a word of thanks for their work.

Every member who is absent should receive a telephone call or a personal visit or a note telling her she was missed and recapturing one or two of the highlights of that meeting.

23. Never ask anyone in a large group meeting to remain seated in the same chair for more than ninety minutes without a break. Motion picture theaters can expect 100 to 130 minutes from patrons, but these customers usually are seated in well-upholstered chairs, the pace is fast, the communication is largely visual, and humor and/or suspense and/or

popcorn help the time go by rapidly. In addition, a large proportion of movie-goers are under thirty.

24. Just before the benediction is pronounced, thank everyone for coming, make sure that expression of gratitude is accompanied by a smile and a brief statement on why they will want to be sure to attend next month's meeting.

Finally, always adjourn at least two minutes before the time called for in the advance publicity or the agenda.

These are some of the central principles that can be useful in planning and conducting large group meetings. It should be remembered that many of the principles that are useful in small group dynamics often are counterproductive when utilized in large group meetings.

One example is the circle. A circle often is the most productive seating arrangement for small groups but should not be utilized when the number of participants exceeds thirty. In the small group that gathering of people is

Seating arrangements help determine the size of our attendance!
—FRIAR TUCK

Large groups need a focal point around which to center their attention!
— FRIAR TUCK

WOW! SHE'S SMART, PERSUASIVE, AND KNOWS WHERE WE'RE GOING!

A prepared agenda and a competent leader are necessities at a large meeting!

— FRIAR TUCK

the focal point of everyone's attention. That is one reason to use a seating arrangement that facilitates eye contact. By contrast, the large group needs a clearly defined and attractive focal point for everyone's attention. In worship, that may be the chancel or the pulpit. At the monthly general meeting, that may be a speaker's table or a display that is the focal point of the discussion.

A second difference is that a small group can meet for two and one-half hours without a break but that is too long for a large group. A third is that frequently the leadership of the small group is in the group and the agenda can be surfaced in that meeting. Large groups need an agenda that is prepared in advance, but it can be amended or revised. Likewise large groups need a designated and competent leader who is willing to accept that leadership role.

It is possible, and often wise, to utilize small group principles in organizing the circles in the women's organization, but large group organizing principles always should be followed in planning and conducting that monthly general meeting. One effective means of keeping the attendance low is to run it like a family reunion or assume it can be run as an overgrown small group. If the goal is to include fifty to one hundred or more women at those monthly general meetings, it will be useful to plan and organize it as a large group event.

In summary, a common question is, Should those monthly general meetings be used to reinforce loyalties to circles, or should the members' loyalties to their circles be expected to motivate them to attend the monthly general meeting?

The best answer is yes and no.

Yes, one purpose of those monthly general meetings can be to lift up the merits of each circle and to help reinforce circle loyalties. Asking each circle to take responsibility for one monthly general meeting can be one means of accomplishing that. No, it is somewhere between unrealistic and naive to expect loyalty to a particular circle to motivate a person to attend the general meetings. Both the circles and the general meetings have to offer reasons to people for making the effort to attend, but these can be mutually reinforcing.

In other words, that monthly general meeting can reinforce women's loyalty to both their circle and to the larger fellowship, but it is asking too much to expect loyalty to a particular circle to motivate members to attend that monthly general meeting. It must stand on its own merits, not rely on the circles, to attract participants.

CHAPTER FIVE

Forty-Two Other Ways

While it may not be the easiest choice to implement, the most effective single approach to revitalizing the women's organization in your church probably will be to find a committed, skilled, aggressive, creative, and persistent new leader who will make this the central cause in her life for the next several years. Susan Brown is one example of such a leader.

A second possibility, as suggested in the previous chapter, could be to begin by organizing those monthly general meetings around large group principles and make them more attractive events.

Create New Entry Points

A third, which was a big component of the strategy followed at Trinity Church, is to create a series of attractive new entry points that can enable the women's fellowship to appeal to and to accommodate new members. This parallels the most effective means of revitalizing any long-established organization, which is to attract a new generation of new members.

This is raised early in this chapter because it can be a highly divisive approach. This takes us back to a fundamental policy question raised in the first chapter. What is the *primary* purpose of the women's organization? Is it primarily and largely a missionary organization designed to give women the opportunity to learn more about missions, to become more active in supporting missions around the world, and to become actively involved in doing ministry beyond the

106

bounds of that organization? Or should it be seen in larger terms as a women's organization that is concerned with a broad agenda including world-wide missions?

Or does a middle ground exist that enables this both to be a missionary society and to challenge women with a broad range of opportunities to be engaged in doing ministry, including some that do not fit under the traditional umbrella of missions?

This is a critical policy question. The answer to

SOMEHOW...WE ALL FIT INTO ALL OF THIS!

Is our range of possibilities in ministry broad enough to include the gifts of all our women?

—FRIAR TUCK.

that question will provide part of the context for evaluating many of the alternatives listed below. The answer to that policy question also will influence which new entry points will be acceptable and which will be challenged as inconsistent with the role of a single purpose missionary society.

Before moving on to a range of alternatives, it may be useful to offer a dozen suggestions on creating new entry points for potential new members.

1. Recognize that more people will be interested in helping pioneer the new, but fewer will display interest in joining a long-established organization or group.

2. Do not depend on a single invitation. Use a redundant system for inviting potential new members.

3. A person is more likely to respond affirmatively if the focus of the group overlaps a need of that individual.

4. Most of us find it easier to venture into a new place if we are accompanied by a friend or acquaintance, so encourage members to offer to pick up and bring that potential new member.

GUESS WHAT?
I'M ON THE AGENDA!

We respond
when the group's
focus overlaps
with our needs!

—FRIAR TUCK

WE'RE ON THE SAME
VOLLEYBALL TEAM...
I'M THE WATER-PERSON!

Social settings
and common tasks
are the best ways
to meet new friends!

—FRIAR TUCK

5. As a general rule most adults find it easier to meet and make new friends in either (a) a social setting or (b) a common task that requires additional people to complete it (replacing the front steps of that widow's house or a mission work-camp trip or preparing and serving a meal or rehearsing a play or participating in a quilting group). Most of us find it more difficult to meet and make new friends at a worship service or at a business meeting.

6. Be sure some of your members will be present early to meet and welcome newcomers and to help make the new circle or the new task force a successful experience.

7. Do not put all your eggs in one basket. Offer people choices and do not be disappointed if some of your new entry points fail to attract any responses.

8. Do not underestimate the value of refreshments at that first gathering!

9. Ask someone to accept responsibility for that first gathering who will be able to give that meeting a sense of purpose, move-

ment, and accomplishment so people leave feeling glad they came.

10. If you choose a broad umbrella for the definition for the role of your women's fellowship, be sure that at least one or two members who have had a personal experience with the narrowly defined focal point for that particular circle be part of the nucleus for that circle.

Thus if this is a new circle for mothers of developmentally disabled children, one or two of your members who are helping

LADIES, LET ME TELL YOU ABOUT OUR NEW SUNDAY AFTERNOON CIRCLE OF TV FOOTBALL WIDOWS!

Those who would organize a new circle need to have experience with its reason for meeting!
—FRIAR TUCK

create this new group should be mothers of developmentally disabled children. If that new circle is to be created for women who now operate their own businesses, choose a couple of successful entrepreneurial types as the core leaders in organizing it. If you plan to create a new group for women who have been widowed, you need a couple of widows who have learned how to respond to widowhood as the initial organizers. If you expect to organize a new circle for new mothers who are combining a full-time job with motherhood, select a couple of good role models to serve as the organizing leaders. If you plan to create a new mutual support group for women who have experienced an unhappy recovery from a hysterectomy, that new group should include a couple of women who have moved beyond the trauma of that unhappy experience, but sympathetically understand the feelings of those who are experiencing it.

11. Be prepared to announce the time, place, and purpose of the next meeting before adjourning that first gathering.

12. If you expect fewer than ten or twelve people at that

TONIGHT, WE'RE GOING TO TALK ABOUT TOGETHERNESS!

Arrange your seating to meet your purpose!

—FRIAR TUCK

first meeting and if this is to be a "business" gathering, arrange the chairs around one large table or two tables that have been pushed together. If the agenda is personal concerns, arrange the chairs in an open circle. If you expect more than seventeen or eighteen at that first meeting, it may be useful to arrange the chairs in rows and have the convener and one or two other people seated at a table when the meeting begins or to meet in a large living room setting where there are comfortable chairs around the perimeter of the room.

If you expect ten to seventeen people, a living room arrangement in a home or in the church parlor may be the appropriate seating arrangement.

A National and Regional Support System

What is the primary role of the regional and national offices in relating to the women's fellowship in local churches? Is it to organize a separate and distinctive worldwide missionary effort that will challenge, inspire, and evoke the support of the women in pews back home? Or is it to challenge women to a new view of the world and of the Christian's responsibilities in that world? Is it to provide the study materials to motivate women to support what is now a denominationally administered worldwide missions program? Is it to challenge both the women in the pews back home and denominational leaders (mostly male) to respond to new opportunities in ministry and outreach. Should the national office be expected to serve as a lobby in support of feminist causes and seek to enlist support from the women back home? Or should the national and regional offices place a high priority in programming such as retreats, rallies, and mission study tours?

It can be argued this question belongs in the first chapter along with twenty other policy questions. It is placed here because this can be one avenue for revitalizing the women's fellowship in local churches.

IF WE DON'T NOURISH THE ROOTS WE'LL NEVER ENJOY THE TREE!

National and regional offices can encourage local growth!

—FRIAR TUCK

One of the reasons for the existence of regional and national offices in the women's organization could be to help strengthen the local units. In addition to offering a channel for local support of worldwide efforts in missions and evangelism and providing study materials, these denominational agencies might (1) conduct regional workshops on leadership skills for newly elected officers, (2) help arrange mission work-camp trips, (3) schedule both regional and national inspirational rallies, (4) provide manuals and offer workshops on small group dynamics for circle leaders and on large group dynamics for those responsible for that monthly general meeting, (5) offer suggestions on new member enlistment, (6) offer specific suggestions on how to organize new circles or interest groups, (7) suggest new ventures for direct involvement in doing ministry for women in local units, (8) arrange annual visits to specific mission ventures in various states and provinces, (9) conduct an annual school on missions designed both to challenge and to inform women on today's opportunities, (10) publish a newsletter focused on the agenda, concerns, and problems of local leaders (in contrast to the denominational magazine that often tends to reflect a "headquarters perspective," (11) schedule regular field visits to listen to the concerns of women from the local units, and (12) conduct workshops on how to reach new generations of women and identify one or two "teaching churches" in each of several states. (These teaching churches could explain to overnight visitors what they did and how they did it as they revitalized the women's fellowship in that parish. The teaching church could both host and staff a variety of training events.)

Open the Door Wider

One of the policy questions that will affect the size of the women's organization in most congregations concerns criteria for membership. Is membership in the local unit restricted to women who are members of that congregation? Or is the door open a bit more so that the woman who is a member of Church A (which may not have a women's fellowship or it may include only mature women or it may not be receptive to new agendas) may become a member of the women's organization in Church B? What if these congregations represent two different denominations? In several denominations a woman must be a member of a congregation of that denomination to serve as an officer or to be eligible to be a delegate to regional or national conventions.

One side of this debate insists that congregational membership is a prerequisite for holding any office in that parish. "You don't expect us to let nonmembers run our church, do you?"

The other side places a higher priority on the role of the women's fellowship as an entry point for future new members and encourages women to join the women's organization as a part of their introduction to that congregation before they formally unite with that parish.

This inclusionary perspective also recognizes and accepts as a fact of life that today several million Christians on the North American continent actively participate in the life of two or more congregations week after week.

One example is the woman who worships on Sunday

morning with her aging parents in the congregation where she grew up, where her parents have been members for a half century, where all of their surviving friends are members, and where several of her friends and many of her acquaintances worship. She may even provide the transportation for her parents to get to church and back home every week. Sunday evening she may attend worship in a church of another denomination where she finds that worship experience meets her religious needs. Twice a month or perhaps weekly she may be an active member of a women's Bible study group sponsored by a third church. Every spring she joins several friends in a drama group in a fourth church that offers a superb religious drama the first weekend in May. Which of these congregations should feel free to extend an invitation to her to join their women's fellowship? Could she become a member and perhaps even become an officer if she is not a member of that parish?

A second, and far more common example, is the woman who has been a leader of the women's fellowship in her "home church" in Iowa for the past twenty years. Three years ago when her husband retired, they purchased a small winter home in New Mexico where they spend four or five months of the year. Their denomination either does not have a church in that community or it repelled them on their first visit. As a result they are now active participants in another church in New Mexico of a different denomination. This congregation has a relatively small resident membership and is seeking to expand the organizational life during the months the snowbirds are in town. The women's organization in this congregation is short of skilled and enthusiastic leaders. Can they ask this woman to join? Can she become an officer? Or must she first ask for her membership to be transferred to this congregation from her home church in Iowa? Or can she become an officer if she becomes an "affiliate" member of that parish?

A third and increasingly common example is the woman who was reared in a Roman Catholic home and grew up to become a devout Catholic. She married a Protestant and they agreed not to expect the other to change religious affiliation.

After attending Mass every Sunday morning, she attends worship with her husband in a Protestant church. Can she become an active member of the women's fellowship in that Protestant congregation?

How restrictive should you be in your requirements for membership? For becoming an officer or a delegate? The simplest answer is to require membership in that congregation before one can become a member of the women's fellowship and accept the tradeoff that this may mean fewer members. The compromise of, "Yes, you can become a member and work on our projects, but you cannot be an officer unless you are a member of this parish," is less and less acceptable to women born after 1945.

How wide are you prepared to open that door for potential new members? Is it reasonable to expect someone coming from a different denominational tradition to be able to offer some creative leadership, even if she is not prepared to ask for her church membership to be transferred? Or do you place a higher priority on the necessity of her first being accepted as a full member of that congregation?

One side may contend that active leadership in that congregation is prerequisite to becoming an officer in the women's fellowship. The other side argues that the women's fellowship can be excellent preparation for women who eventually will hold influential elective positions in that parish. Which side of the argument do you believe is the most persuasive? Is your women's fellowship strictly an auxiliary organization of that congregation? Or can it be an entry point for future new members? Should entrance into the women's fellowship be subsequent to taking the vows of membership in that parish? Or is it acceptable to become a member of the women's fellowship before uniting with that congregation?

Attend That National Rally

If the decision is to make missions the central purpose of this women's fellowship, one of the most effective means of revitalizing that local unit is to take seven to twenty women, including at least a couple of potential new members if at all possible, to that *national* rally sponsored by the women's organization of your denomination.

A second best alternative is for a group, again including potential new members if at all possible, to attend a *regional* rally sponsored by your denomination.

This also can be a productive experience even if you have decided to build a broad umbrella over the statement of purpose of your local unit. With rare exceptions this is one of the best rallying points for bringing together a group of Christians and inspiring them to seek a greater degree of involvement in ministry and outreach.

Like several of the other suggestions offered in this chapter, that trip to the national rally can be a highly productive shared experience that helps reinforce a sense of common purpose, unity, and cohesion. The stranger who goes along will return a few days later not only with a new vision of what could be, but also with several new close friends.

Women's national offices function better when separated from denominational headquarters!

—FRIAR TUCK

Attending national and regional meetings together can be an effective means of assimilation!

—FRIAR TUCK

Rear Your Own Replacements

"We simply cannot attract younger women!" is a common complaint from the mature leaders of the women's fellowship in hundreds of congregations.

One response, as suggested earlier in this chapter, is to create more attractive new entry points for new generations of members. A second alternative is illustrated by the organizational structure of the Woman's Missionary Union of the Southern Baptist Convention. In 1987 nearly one-half of their total membership was under thirty years of age! That statement will startle many readers.

The explanation is that for generations a central feature of the Woman's Missionary Union (WMU) has been to inculcate in children and youth the importance of worldwide missions. A fringe benefit of this tremendous emphasis on missionary education has been what one outsider described as a system for "growing their own future leaders."

In programmatic terms this means that one programmatic unit of the WMU is Missions Friends which is designed for girls age 5 and younger. In 1987, it enrolled 173,572 preschool girls, up from 119,314 in 1973. Those who demand a Biblical explanation for this practice may want to read Proverbs 22:6. Those who seek a modern defense can turn to the research in early childhood development theory, which suggests that as much as one-half of an adult's character is formed during the first four years of life.

A second component of the WMU is Girls in Action for girls age 6 to 11, which enrolled 226,880 preteens in 1987, up from 215,750 in 1973. The third is Acteens for girls age 12-17 and a fourth is Baptist Young Women for women in the 18-29 age bracket.

One alternative for strengthening the future of the women's organization in your church is to rear your own replacements.

This approach requires (a) a long time frame for planning, (b) an assumption the world will not come to an end in the near future, (c) a well-organized and relevant denominational support system to provide leadership and other resources, (d) a long-term commitment to missions as the central organizing principle (one of the few themes that can win the active support of all ages), (e) widespread and consistent agreement from generation to generation on the operational definition of missions, (f) a deep conviction that education in general and missionary education in particular can be influential in shaping an individual's values, priorities, and practices, (g) an excellent leadership training program to provide competent leadership for those groups of young girls, and (h) an operational and institutional adoption of the concept that one way to motivate children is to teach deferred gratification, to give them something to look forward to a few years hence ("I can't wait until I'm old enough to be a member of that group"), and to design a system rich in symbols, a sense of accomplishment, progress, and satisfactions.

What do you see as the

ANY SMART PASTOR KNOWS THAT A STRONG WOMEN'S GROUP MAKES OUR WORK LIGHTER!

— FRIAR TUCK•

ONCE YOU'VE BEEN THERE, LIFE IS FOREVER CHANGED BACK WHERE YOU CAME FROM!

Mission work-camp trips can create greater inner growth than a dozen study groups!

— FRIAR TUCK•

primary source of the leaders in your women's organization forty years from now? How old are those leaders today? What are they doing? Who is preparing them for leadership responsibilities in your women's organization in the year 2035?

Plan a Mission Work-Camp Trip

While some denominations discourage this, the closest to a guaranteed route to (a) the revitalization of that local women's fellowship and (b) reinforcing and expanding the support for missions in that entire congregation is to encourage seven to thirty adults to spend a week or two in a mission work-camp experience with a group of Christians on another continent. These tend to have a greater impact if (a) a period of several months of study and preparation precedes the trip, (b) English is not the native language of the people to be visited, (c) the visitors and their hosts actually work together (building a chapel, run-

ning a dental clinic, and
vaccinating children are
three common examples),
and (d) a period of reflection, debriefing, discus-
sion, and sharing is scheduled following the return.

Four of the more com-
mon products of such a
visit are (a) a deeper recognition of the many bless-
ings the people on this continent enjoy and a greater
sense of gratitude for these
blessings, (b) the people
who return are changed
individuals, (c) the participants cannot help sharing
their new and deeper com-

mitment to missions with others, and (d) that commitment is
contagious.

The missionary on furlough may come, preach, show
slides, stir up interest, and depart the next day. These folks
stay and reinforce the urgency of missions among the people
of that congregation day after day, week after week, and
month after month.

Advertise!

If creating new entry points for potential future new
members ranks high on the list of ways to revitalize the
women's fellowship, it logically follows that inviting people to
share in these new ministries also must be a high priority. As
was mentioned briefly in chapter 3, this was a high priority
for Susan Brown and she won the greater use of direct mail
advertising to reach prospective new members.

Direct mail can be a useful, and relatively cost-efficient
means of identifying potential new members for new circles,
programs, and ministries.

One example is the visit to the county courthouse to secure the names and addresses of all women who gave birth to a baby during the past several months. Each one receives a first-class envelope that contains one sheet of paper. At the top of that sheet is this question in large type:

ARE YOU HOME ALL DAY WITH A NEW BABY?

If you are, come and join other new mothers next Tuesday morning at 10:30 A.M. at Prescott Road Church. Bring your sack lunch. We'll provide a choice of beverages and a chance for you to meet several other new mothers. Our luncheon speaker will be Dr. Soandso, a pediatrician who will talk with us about our parenting questions. We plan to adjourn by 2:00 P.M.

A second paragraph should offer more details including location of the church.

Ideally, the third paragraph will include the names, addresses, and telephone numbers of three or four mothers who constitute the organizing team for this new group.

While this can be a form letter, each one is individually signed by the sender followed by a handwritten postscript such as, "If you need a ride, call me at 347-8109" or "If you have questions, feel free to call me at 347-8109."

This letter should be on 6 × 9 inch personal stationery, not a church letterhead, mailed in a 3½ × 6½ inch personal size envelope with the name and address of the sender, not the church's name and address, in the upper left-hand corner, the name and address of the recipient should be either handwritten or typed (no labels) and a colorful first-class commemorative stamp should be placed in the upper right-hand corner of the envelope. (Do not use a postage meter or coil stamps!)

Similar letters can be mailed to invite potential new members to help pioneer other new groups and to newcomers to the community. A response rate of 1 to 2 percent for direct mail advertising is considered to be very good, so a thousand letters (three hundred dollars for postage, paper, and envelopes) may produce ten to twenty potential new members.

This is one means of reaching beyond today's membership to create new circles, groups, and programs. Other channels may include thirty-minute spot announcements on the local radio station, a "news story" in the weekly paper, an ad in the "shopper throwaway," posters, telephone calls, a notice in the parish newsletter and the Sunday morning bulletin, a notice on the bulletin board at the supermarket or in that office building that houses hundreds of working women, an interview on

"Direct mail can be a useful, and relatively cost-efficient means of identifying potential new members."
—FRIAR TUCK

the local radio station during the rush hour, a notice on the community bulletin board, two or three four-line ads scattered in the classified advertising section of the newspaper, a big sign on the bulletin board out in front of the church building, and monthly announcements in other local women's organizations.

A realistic goal is for a women's fellowship to spend five to ten dollars times the membership on advertising every year if the goal is to reach beyond today's church members to add new members to that organization.

Obviously the decision on advertising MUST be made after a decision has been made on whether or not women who are not (yet?) members of that congregation will be welcome. Do not invite strangers and reject them because they are not members of that parish!

Create the Matthew 25:35 Circle

A new circle can be organized in response to the command of Jesus in Matthew 25:35—to feed the hungry,' clothe the naked, and visit those in prison.

This is clearly an action circle dedicated to helping those in need. It may focus on sheltering the homeless or on providing clothes for the needy or visiting those in prison or on building and filling bird feeders outside the windows of residents of nursing homes,[2] or caring for shutins or creating a home for battered women or organizing mutual support groups for parents with children who have AIDS or responding to some urgent but widely neglected need.

These circles tend to attract a disproportionately large number of (a) younger women, (b) mature women, (c) people seeking a structured opportunity to express their commitment to Jesus Christ as Lord and Savior, and (d) wives of husbands who travel.

These circles almost always are exceptionally open and receptive to new members. One reason is the leaders often respond to challenges that are beyond the resources of the original group and additional help is always welcome.

Should You Staff It?

Perhaps one of the two or three most controversial alternatives in this chapter reflects a course of action followed by a tiny proportion of congregations. This is to hire someone, usually a woman on a part-time basis, to staff the women's fellowship. The most common analogy cited in defense of this decision was the hiring, many years ago, of a director of Christian education to pick up part of the work load that had been carried for decades by the volunteer Sunday school superintendent. A second parallel is the staff person to work with youth. A third precedent is the paid staff person in the regional or national office of the women's organization in that denomination, again to pick up part of the work load previously carried by volunteers.

While the number of local women's fellowships who have employed a staff person remains relatively tiny, these experiences have produced some instructive questions.

1. Should this new staff member be (a) selected and paid by the women's fellowship and accountable to the executive committee or (b) chosen to be a member of the program staff

of that congregation and assigned to work with the women's fellowship or (c) selected by and accountable to the pastor or (d) some other arrangement? (Historically, the most common example of a response to this need was the pastor's wife who came and became the unpaid executive secretary of the local women's fellowship.)

2. Should this staff member be perceived and function as (a) an administrative secretary for the women's fellowship working under the oversight of the volunteer president and/or the executive committee or (b) a program specialist to create, enlist, and train the volunteer staff necessary for those new programs or (c) a specialist in missions and outreach who will concentrate her energy on opening new doors for more women to be involved in missions, outreach, and community ministries?

3. Should this person be paid (a) out of the operating budget of that congregation or (b) out of the missions budget or (c) out of the treasury of the women's fellowship or (d) from second-mile designated giving?

The results suggest that if a person can be found who (a) can get along with the pastor and other staff members, (b) will motivate, enlist, train, and work with volunteers, (c) is able to see and develop programmatic responses to unmet needs, (d) is sensitive to the differences among people including generational differences, (e) displays a passion for missions, and (f) is an energetic, venturesome, and creative individual, this can be a remarkably effective means of revitalizing that women's fellowship, enlisting a new generation of younger women, expanding the definition of and support for missions, and enhancing the morale of the women's fellowship.

Maintain Your Own Headquarters

For others the most controversial suggestion in this book concerns the organizational and geographical location of the national headquarters.

Although it is impossible to prove a direct cause-and-effect relationship and no one factor can be singled out as decisive, experience suggests the national denominational office of the women's organization will be more effective in servicing its constituency if it is (a) an auxiliary rather than an integral part of the national denominational structure and (b) not located in the same city as other national agencies of that denomination. Many students of organizational theory will see this as a self-evident proposition.

Opponents usually offer such arguments as efficiency, economy, better internal and interagency communication, easier coordination of programs and schedules, cooperation, easier access by the constituency (one can visit several offices in one trip to the same address), and an image of cooperation as reasons for integrating the national office for the women's organization into the large denominational structure.

This organizational and geographical incorporation of the national headquarters of the women's organization into the national offices of that denomination also can be seen as consistent with the evolution of the social movement into a respectable formal organization in which means-to-an-end concerns float to the top of the agenda.

Experience suggests a separate office that is not organizationally a part of the national denominational structure and that is located in a different city (a) helps the women's organization maintain its own distinctive identity and role and reinforces its role as an auxiliary, (b) minimizes a blurring of that central purpose, (c) reduces the chances that the women's organization will be diverted from that central purpose by denominational quarrels over power and priorities, (d) largely eliminates the temptation for nepotism, (e) isolates it at least in part from the temptation by other denominational agencies to turn to the women's organization to "help us solve our problems" and thus divert resources from that central purpose, (f) enables the women's organization to escape the negative feelings that many local church leaders have toward "national headquarters," (g) makes it much easier for the women's organization to justify the necessity of having its own magazine, its own mailing list, and its own direct mail contacts with its own constituency rather than "cooperating" in a general mailing effort to all the churches in which that distinctive message can be lost, (h) almost completely eliminates proposals that the members of the advisory board of the national women's organization should be selected by males attending that denomination's national conference, (i) will provide some useful "wiggle room" when potentially divisive issues surface in a denominational political scene (such as the choice of the next chief executive officer of that denomination or the next presiding officer), (j) reduces the opportunities for other leaders and agencies in the national denominational structure to accept the role of a veto block as they seek to tell others what they cannot do, (k) usually will result in lower annual dollar costs, and (l) perhaps most significant, makes it more likely that the national office will be a source of relevant and creative suggestions designed for congregational leaders.

In summary, if the national office of the women's organization is both organizationally and geographically a part of the national headquarters of that denomination, it will be easy to drift into a stance that views the national headquarters as the number-one client. If the national office is both organizationally and geographically separate, it is far easier to concentrate on the central purpose and on the women in local churches as the number-one constituency of that agency.

For many of the smaller denominations the best alternative may be to house the national headquarters in the home of that part-time employee who serves as the only paid national staff person for the women's organization of that denomination.

Offer Bible Study

Although accurate comparative statistics are not available, a reasonable guess is that Bible Study Fellowship (BSF) has enrolled more women in serious, structured, intensive, and extensive Bible study than any other contemporary approach to adult Bible study on the North American continent.

At least four reasons can be cited for the phenomenal spread of this program. One is the design of the program including the teaching training component. A second is it is a "high expectation" program and today, as in centuries past, Christians do respond affirmatively to high expectations. A third reason is it was designed to respond to the questions thousands of women have about the Holy Scriptures. Finally, it filled a vacuum.

One reason that vacuum existed is long-established congregations have not been offering the type of Bible study women sought. Bible Study Fellowship identified the need and filled it.

The moral of that story is one of the most effective possibilities for a women's fellowship to reach larger numbers of people is through a high quality, demanding, carefully structured, and attractive Bible study program taught by competent teachers. This can be an especially productive means of reaching women born after 1945. More women are members of serious Bible study groups that meet on a weekly basis than ever before in American history, and a disproportionately large number are women born after World War II. For many local fellowships the attractiveness of this alternative can be enhanced by active support from denominational headquarters. Other congregations will find it easier to act unilaterally.

Organize a Mother's Club

Millions of American women have gone straight from school to join the labor force and have postponed motherhood until their late twenties or early thirties. The number of women giving birth to their first child after the mother's thirtieth birthday more than doubled between 1960 and 1988, despite the decrease in the total number of births.

Many of these women learned to meet and make friends at work, unlike their mothers who met and made friends from among the neighbors. Despite the publicity given to the need for institutional child care facilities for children of mothers employed outside the home, in 1988 the American population included nearly six million married women with one or more children at home under six years of age, who were not employed outside the home, even on a part-time basis. That is a sharp drop from the eleven million mothers who fit that category in 1960, but six million is still a big number. In addition, many of those seven million married women who are in the labor force and who have one or more children under age six at home either work nights or work out of their home or hold what are less than full-time jobs.

If one focuses in more sharply on mothers of young children, according to the United States Bureau of Labor Statistics, in 1988 55 percent of mothers of children under age three were not employed outside the home and another 20 percent worked only on a part-time basis or seasonally. In other words, a huge number of mothers are home all day with a baby or a one-year-old or a two-year-old.

Hundreds of churches have discovered these statistics add up to the need for a club for mothers of young children. Sometimes the group includes mothers who are not currently married as well as mothers with husbands.

Seven of the most common organizing principles for creating a mother's club are (1) the opportunity to meet and make new friends, (2) serious weekly Bible study, (3) exercise classes, (4) enrollment of one or more of the children of that mother in the weekday early childhood development center operated by that church, (5) sewing classes that enable mothers to learn to sew, (6) the chance to learn parenting skills and to share experiences, and (7) for some the most attractive feature is participation in what becomes a mutual support group. This last feature is mentioned most frequently by (a) single parent mothers, (b) mothers who have left the labor force after many years to stay home and rear a family, and (c) mothers without any kinfolk or longtime friends in that community. (It is not uncommon today for the pregnant wife who accompanies her husband to his new job in a different community to decide not to continue in the labor force since the baby is due in a few months. Thus she finds herself in a new community without friends or relatives. The mother's club provides not only a chance to meet and make new friends, but also may offer a mutual support group for that new mother who has mixed feelings about giving up her career to rear a family—while the husband finds it easy to meet and make new friends at work and enjoys the continuity and identity of that job.)

Some may argue that creation of a mother's club is not an appropriate responsibility for the women's fellowship—especially if it sees itself as strictly a missionary society. A few will contend that it is better for that congregation not to offer a mother's club than to have the women's fellowship take the responsibility for organizing it. Others will declare, "If that's needed, someone else should organize it, not us."

On the other side of this debate are those who see the mother's club as an attractive entry point for a new generation of younger women into the women's organization, who are convinced it is a good response to a real need, who are willing to expand the umbrella over the women's organization to include it, who are convinced many of these mothers eventually will become enthusiastic converts to the cause of missions, and who worry more about being responsive to contemporary needs than overstepping institutional boundaries.

How do you feel about this debate?

What About a Women's Chorale?

Another example of the debate over how broad the umbrella should be is illustrated by the line that divides the women's fellowship from the music program. Does the music program in your congregation include a women's vocal group?

If it does not, you may want to consider expanding the women's organization by organizing a women's chorale.

In one congregation a leader described this circle in the women's fellowship as a group who "joyously share their faith through song, enthusiastically witness to Christ as their Savior by bringing music to small congregations that do not have a choir, to nursing homes, to senior citizens' gatherings, to denominational meetings, and to ecumenical occasions."

A member of this group explained, "A good voice and the ability to carry a tune are two of the gifts God gave to me. Singing enables me to use these gifts to inspire others, to express my love for music, to witness to my faith, to uplift those who need what we can bring."

DID THEY SAY I WAS TO SING BASS OR THAT MY SINGING WAS VERY BASE ?

A mutual love of music can bring together very different kinds of folks !

— FRIAR TUCK.

Music groups also possess four distinctive characteristics that should not be overlooked. This may be the easiest way we have to bring people together across generational lines. Marital status is not a factor in determining who feels a sense of belonging. It usually is remarkably easy for a new person to join and become assimilated into a music group. Finally, music overcomes barriers of race, nationality, and social class very quickly.

Should you urge that the music program in your church be expanded to include a women's chorale? Or do you want to offer this as a part of the total program and outreach of your women's fellowship? This can be one of the most effective means of reaching women who are not members of your congregation.

Schedule a Bazaar

"About ten years ago the Session voted to prohibit all money-making activities," explained a member of the women's organization at Westminster Presbyterian Church to a new member. "The only exception is the high school youth group is allowed to have three money-raising events every year."

"The reason I asked," explained the forty-seven-year-old member, "is that in the church we came from, the bazaar was

WITH SUCH A PROVEN
TRACK RECORD
WHO WOULD EVER WANT
TO GET OFF THE TRACK
BY DROPPING IT?

The worth of a bazaar
can be measured annually!

—FRIAR TUCK

the big annual event for the women's organization. It was the number-one rallying point for the women. It was an exciting event, and a lot of us looked forward every year to that third week in October when the bazaar was held. Some of us were convinced it generated more enthusiasm, more excitement, greater participation, and more interest than anything else that happened in the church during the rest of the year."

"While that wasn't a big factor, it was one of the reasons our Session voted to prohibit any money-raising activities here," explained the first woman. "Some felt that our bazaar had gotten too big. It had become the tail that wagged the dog. Another factor was that a lot of our women were getting tired. A bazaar is a lot of work, and with so many women employed outside the home today, that meant most of the burden fell on a smaller and smaller number of people. The big reason, however, was that the minister who was here at the time believed very strongly that a congregation should support all of its ministries and programs, including missions, out of the offering plate. A lot of us agreed that money-making activities undercut the whole concept of stewardship. Personally, while I do miss it, I'm glad we made the decision we did."

"How many circles do you have here at Westminster?" asked the newcomer.

"We did have five, but one disbanded about six or seven years ago and last year we merged two of the smaller circles, so we are down to three," came the reply. "All three are study groups, one meets in the morning, one in the afternoon, and one in the evening."

"WOMEN FROM OUTSIDE THE CHURCH NEED TO FEEL WELCOME!"

- FRIAR TUCK

"The church we came from is smaller than this congregation and we had seven circles," commented the newcomer. "We had a morning circle for mothers of young children, three study circles, one of which met in the evening, plus three other evening circles. I became convinced that getting ready for the bazaar was a big factor in what kept all those groups going. In addition to their study program and fellowship, they had a goal. That goal was to raise money for missions. That wasn't their only reason for being, but it was a big factor."

"Oh, we raise money for missions," replied the first woman somewhat defensively, "but instead of doing it through dinners or a bazaar, we do it with pledges. Each woman makes an annual pledge for missions. Last year these pledges brought in nearly a thousand dollars for missions."

"We did that, too," retorted the newcomer, "but at our bazaar we also cleared between two and three thousand dollars every year for missions in addition to the pledges."

This conversation reflects several of the arguments used in defense of or in opposition to the idea of the annual bazaar sponsored by the women's organization. This conversation, however, overlooks two other aspects of the bazaar that merit consideration.

Every congregation should be concerned about the entry points for newcomers. How do new members or prospective new members gain a sense of belonging? How do we assimilate new people into our church? How do we enable new members to take that second step that carries them from being members of the congregation into feeling as if they belong to our fellowship?

Perhaps the best example of this is the choir organized around vocal music. (Some choirs are organized around fellowship and may become exclusionary groups.) In most churches the newcomer who is a good tenor immediately is welcomed into the choir and quickly gains a sense of belonging. This sequence illustrates the old adage, "You know you belong when you know you are needed."

A second example of this same dynamic is illustrated by the congregation that decides to construct, largely with volunteer labor, a badly needed addition to its meeting place. The new member who is a skilled carpenter and who is a willing volunteer soon gains a sense of belonging.

A third illustration of entry points is the bazaar. The new member, who may feel a bit out of place when she joins a study circle two or three months after that group has embarked on a new study program, may find helping prepare for the bazaar an easy and attractive entry into that fellowship. Frequently, study groups tend to become exclusionary after the first or second meeting. By contrast, any group organized around completion of a task that requires more hands usually is very open to newcomers. In many churches the annual bazaar is the number-one entry point for new members into the women's organization.

A second reason why a bazaar deserves serious consideration is that it illustrates some concepts that apply to many other organizations ranging from a Men's Fellowship to Vacation Bible School. Why does it work?

One reason has been mentioned. It often is a wide open entry point for newcomers. A second reason the bazaar works is the obvious emphasis on enlisting volunteers around a terminal date. You know in advance when your obligation will be fulfilled. It is easier to find someone who will help move a table than it is to find someone who will teach a Sunday school class forever. We all like to know when our obligation will be completed.

A third reason the bazaar works is because it has a big

demand for people to
express their creative skills
through their hands rather
than simply expressing
creativity via verbal skills.
(This third reason helps
explain why some people
would rather bake bread
or build a bookcase or wash
the car than attend a committee meeting.) The
women's group that is or-
ganized largely around
study (verbal skills) and
fellowship probably will
not attract as many people
as the one organized
around fellowship, study,
and the expression of
creative skills through one's hands.

A fourth reason the bazaar works is that it is designed to
advance a cause, the cause being missions. Every Christian
congregation can count on efforts to advance missions and
outreach as causes that will enhance the vitality of that
church.

A fifth reason the bazaar works is that it is organized
around a specific, attainable, measurable, unifying, and
satisfaction-producing goal—raising money for missions. It is
easy to conclude how well we did, either in comparison with
last year or with this year's goal. For many people the
achievement of goals is a part of how they justify to themselves why they should be part of that particular congregation.

A sixth reason is that the bazaar offers the opportunity for
fun and fellowship. For many, it is a chance to meet and make
new friends, a break in what otherwise may be a dull routine,
an occasion that may be filled with good humor and laughter,
and an excuse to try something new.

A seventh factor is that many of the new members of any

organization feel a need to earn a sense of belonging to that group. After a person has worked hard to help make the bazaar succeed, that person may conclude, "I've paid my dues. I now have a right to belong."

An eighth reason is that it helps the person who works in the bazaar feel, "This is a going outfit. Things do happen here." People prefer to be part of a live and vital program.

Those who feel a strong interest in world missions often raise another issue. "Back when we had a bazaar this church was able to contribute twice as many dollars for missions every year as we do now. After you allow for the impact of inflation, that means we're really doing about a fourth as well as we did when we had a bazaar. One reason for that is the bazaar was our most effective means of keeping the cause of missions before our people. The bazaar really represented the heart of our educational program for missions and now that's gone."

In reflecting on this discussion you may want to ask a half dozen questions.

1. If your congregation has eliminated the bazaar, what has been the replacement as an attractive entry point for newcomers? How do new members gain a sense of belonging?

2. If the governing board in your congregation voted to discontinue the bazaar, does this mean they control the women's fellowship? Or were they simply exercising a legitimate veto power to tell others what they cannot do?

3. What other opportunities, besides a bazaar, does your congregation offer members to express their commitment to

Jesus Christ as Lord and Savior, by expressing their creativity through their hands?

4. How can these basic principles that make a bazaar work be applied to other facets of the women's fellowship?

5. If you now hold the bazaar in the church basement or in the fellowship hall in October or November, would you attract a larger crowd, have more fun, and raise more money if you operated it as an auction under a big tent in August?

WE DON'T HAVE TO WAIT FOR AN EMERGENCY TO USE THEM!

Surrogate grandparents offer a much needed smile and a warm lap!
—FRIAR TUCK

6. Are you taking full advantage of the bazaar as an opportunity for inviting potential future members to participate in it?

The Demand for Surrogate Grandmothers

"We have several mothers who want to drop off their children before seven o'clock, but we simply can't afford to be open that early," explained the director of the day care center to her board at St. James Church. "Our regular hours are from seven in the morning to six in the evening, and we charge parents an overtime fee when they do not come for their children until after six. I suppose we could open at six in the morning and charge an overtime fee for those parents who want to leave their children off early, but somewhere we have to draw a line. We cannot be open twenty-four hours a day."

"How many children would you need to care for before seven?" inquired Hazel Burns, a sixty-seven-year-old leader in the women's fellowship and a charter member of the board for the day care center.

"My guess is only two or three, but if we offer that option, it might increase to a half dozen," replied the director.

"Give me a week, and I'll see what I can do," promised Hazel.

That meeting marked the conception of a new circle. The initial reason for its conception was Hazel's decision to solve the problem at the day care center. She recruited several other grandmothers and organized a schedule that called for two grandmothers to be at the center for an hour early in the morning five days a week. These volunteers provided a loving welcome, a warm lap, a story to be read aloud, and a friendly smile for those children who had to be left off before the official opening hour of seven o'clock.

A year later this was an official and very active circle in the women's fellowship at St. James Church. (Several congregations have organized a parallel surrogate grandfathers' club which is a support group for the weekday nursery school or the athletic program of the church or for an inner-city ministry or the Christian day school or the children's division of the Sunday school.)

Adopt a Seminary Library

For the past several years a combination of the rising costs of books, a budget squeeze, a vast increase in the number of periodicals and scholarly journals, the increase in subscription prices, and the rising costs for staff have forced many of the libraries in theological seminaries to cut back on acquisitions.[3]

A second trend has been the rapidly growing number of the laity who are interested in a serious study of questions on doctrinal, theological, and biblical interpretation issues. One result of this trend has been an increase in the number of religious books sold annually as well as in the number of Christian bookstores. Another has been the formation of adult study groups in churches all across the continent.

A third trend is a product of the erosion of institutional loyalties in general and denominational allegiance in particular. One result is that a growing number of adults find themselves going to church in a religious tradition far different from the one in which they were reared.

Mix these three trends together, shake well, and you may have the ingredients for the creation of a new group in your women's fellowship.

This is a group of venturesome, intellectually curious, and creative women who are interested in new ideas, are comfortable with verbal skills, and are willing to travel.

One example is the circle that adopted the library of a theological seminary as its missions project. Once a year nearly all the women in this circle are guests of the seminary for two days. They sit in on classes, eat in the dining hall, visit with students, get acquainted with the faculty, and spend considerable time with the librarian.

Their regular monthly meetings are organized around (1) discussion of a book all of them have agreed to read, (2) fellowship, (3) mutual support, (4) friendship ties, (5) refreshments, and (6) planning their next big venture. Every spring that venture is the visit to the seminary. During that visit they identify and seek a commitment from the professor who will be the leader for the fall workshop eighteen months later.

Every autumn that big undertaking is a two-day workshop designed for both lay and ministerial leaders from that region. The members of this circle plan it, publicize it, administer it, prepare and serve lunch on both days, and send a check representing the profits to the seminary library. The leader of the workshop is the professor they had secured a commitment from eighteen months earlier. This enables them to publicize next year's theme and speaker at the October workshop as well as mail three thousand brochures in the winter before the coming workshop. With an attendance between two and three hundred at the workshop, this has enabled that circle to send a check for $10,000 to $15,000 to the seminary library year after year.

A PASTOR DOESN'T NEED TO BE CHARISMATIC TO FEEL THE LIFT SPIRIT-FILLED WOMEN CAN BRING TO A CHURCH!

Prayer and praise groups have a place under the umbrella of the women's organization!

FRIAR TUCK

The Charismatic Renewal Circle

While this may threaten many pastors, the charismatic renewal movement is alive and healthy and all the evidence suggests it is continuing to grow in numbers, especially among those born after World War II and among highly educated people working in the fields of science, medicine, and engineering. For a huge variety of reasons many of these self-identified charismatic Christians prefer to be active members of non-charismatic congregations. Some have needs for an experiential worship service that brings charismatic Christians together to worship and praise God in the Tuesday evening prayer and praise service or in the Sunday evening service in a church a few miles away.

Another response, since many of the self-identified charismatic Christians are women who are happily married to a non-charismatic husband who displays zero interest in leaving this congregation to go to an openly charismatic church, is to organize a prayer and praise circle under the umbrella of the women's fellowship. This can be an effective means of encouraging self-identified charismatic Christian women to find a church home that meets their religious needs, even though this is not a charismatic congregation.

At least four factors will be extremely influential in determining the success of this plan. The first, of course, and usually the most powerful, is the pastor's attitude. If the pastor is categorically opposed to the charismatic renewal movement, this becomes a bad idea.

Second is the attitude of the leaders of the women's

fellowship. If they are opposed, the idea probably should be abandoned. If both the pastor and the leaders of the women's fellowship are opposed, it may be wiser to encourage the charismatic members to find a church home where they will be welcome.

Third is the general stance of the congregation. A degree of support for religious diversity is required to make this work. Fourth, the creation of such a circle almost invariably attracts women who

TOGETHER, THEIR PRAYERS MAKE THEIR CARES LIGHTER!

Every church has women who have a need to gather regularly for prayer!

— FRIAR TUCK

are not members of that congregation. If the basic policy decision has been made to exclude women who are not members of that congregation, it probably would be advisable to skip past this alternative.

The Intercessory Prayer Circle

One of the changes experienced in thousands of Protestant congregations on the North American continent during the past three decades is the resurgence of interest in the power of intercessory prayer. This can be seen in the greater emphasis in many churches on that period of intercessory prayer on Sunday morning, in the variety of prayer vigils, in the peace movement, and in the huge response to seminars and workshops on intercessory prayer.

One alternative as you seek to revitalize the women's fellowship in your congregation is to create a new group composed of women who want to be part of a circle organized around the power of intercessory prayer. Some of these groups meet monthly, many meet weekly, and at least a few meet more often.

This can be a tremendous source of comfort, as well as power, for members who want and need someone to pray for them and/or their family members or friends. It also is one of the most effective means of undergirding the spiritual base of the entire congregation.

The Advocacy Circle

This elderly widow has received a formal government letter in regard to her Social Security payment or her Medicare claim. She cannot understand it and does not know what to do.

This husband finally has recognized that his wife, who is afflicted with Alzheimer's disease, is not receiving the care she needs and deserves in the nursing home where she now lives. His daily visits leave him depressed, frustrated, bitter, and feeling completely helpless. What can he do?

This woman preferred charges against the man who raped her. Suddenly she finds herself entangled in a legal system she does not understand and one that makes her feel like the accused rather than the victim. What does she do?

This couple with three children receives an eviction notice that leaves them puzzled, resentful, and frustrated. What do they do?

This mother discovers her son has broken the law and she must appear in court with him next week. What does she do?

This single parent mother just received a notice that she no longer is considered eligible for food stamps. What does she do?

In several communities one alternative is to go to the advocacy committee of a nearby congregation that includes several volunteers with the skills to function as an advocate for persons overwhelmed by the bureaucratic nature of this world.

The rapid increase in the number of women in our society with the professional, technical, and managerial skills needed to serve as an effective advocate deserves attention. The creation of an advocacy circle in the women's fellowship can enable some of these women to be good stewards of these skills by helping those in need.

One of the arguments for creating such a circle in your women's fellowship is that a majority of the victims of this form of bureaucratic oppression are women. Many will find it easier to tell their story to another woman than to cooperate with an adult male. A second argument is this can be an attractive entry point for younger women in your fellowship. A third is it can change the outsider's view of the women's fellowship in your congregation.

What if it works? One of the more common price tags resulting from the success of an advocacy circle is the need for at least a part-time person to be available three or four hours every morning. This may be a volunteer, a paid staff person, or a small group of highly committed volunteers.

This is clearly one of the most challenging and most difficult alternatives to select as you seek to revitalize your organization's relationship with a new generation of women and to respond to the needs of both members and non-members. It also can be one of the most rewarding and satisfaction-producing alternatives.

The Homogeneous Group

In recent years several predominantly Anglo denominations have worked aggressively to become more inclusive. The most notable efforts in this direction include the Assemblies of God, the Southern Baptist Convention, the American Baptist Churches in the U.S.A., the new Evangelical Lutheran Church in America, the Reformed Church in America, the Lutheran Church-Missouri Synod, and the Conservative Baptist Association. Some have been more successful than others in moving in that direction.

The women's organization can be a powerful force in helping congregations become more inclusive. Or, to be more specific, the women's fellowship in your congregation can facilitate the efforts to achieve this goal.

If your congregation exceeds a hundred people at worship, it may be difficult for some people, who feel they do not "belong here," to come and gain a sense of acceptance. The members often insist, "We are a friendly congregation, and everyone is welcome, regardless of race or color or nationality. We welcome everyone who wants to join us in worshiping God."

In fact, however, the nineteen-year-old man reared in rural South Dakota may feel out-of-place walking in on Sunday morning to worship God with an all-Black congregation on Chicago's south side. The Presbyterian who migrated to Canada from Korea a few months ago may feel somewhat out-of-place when walking in to worship with a Presbyterian congregation in Montreal. The young white couple born and reared in Boston may feel out-of-place when they walk in to worship with an all-white congregation of the same denomination in rural Mississippi where only four of those present were born after 1930—and three of those four are children of members back for their annual weekend visit with their aging parents.

One of the more effective means of building an inclusive congregation is to keep it small, to fewer than a hundred at worship. This enables everyone to know everyone else as a person, as an individual child of God. When this small size is reinforced by a strong emphasis on one-to-one relationships, it reduces the tendency to use stereotypes in classifying people.

A second approach is to build a large and inclusive congregation as a federation of homogeneous groups. In effect, this is a congregation of congregations. One variation is to encourage each group to become a small but heterogeneous collection of people where common interests override social, age, gender, ethnic, language, nationality, and class differences. One of the truly redemptive examples is the mutual support group formed for parents who have recently experienced the death of a child. These often attract participants from a huge variety of language, social class, gender, income, racial, ethnic, age, and verbal skill backgrounds.

A more common variation on this theme is the large congregation that includes people from a wide range of backgrounds and viewpoints in terms of age, social class, race, native language, nationality, theological perspective, denominational heritage, and gender. Frequently these churches offer two or three different worship experiences every weekend, sometimes with two different preachers as well as two or three different orders of worship with one in some language other than English. The critical characteristic, however, is in the organizational life. Each of the major organizations is really a federation of homogeneous units. This can be seen in the music program, the athletic or recreational program, the women's organization, the men's fellowship, the adult Sunday school, and the youth program. Each one offers people a wide range of choices.

The women's fellowship, for example, may include a circle composed of mature widows, a second that includes new mothers, a third for women born and reared in Korea, a fourth for women with severe vision handicaps, a fifth for single parent mothers, a sixth for women who have an interfaith marriage, a seventh for women reared in another country who came to the United States as the wife of an American, an eighth for women who share a common interest in drama, a ninth for women who are half of an interracial marriage, a tenth for women born and reared in Cuba or in Mexico or Columbia, an eleventh for women who are members of a mission work-camp group that spends a month on another continent, a twelfth for women who enjoy planning and conducting that annual bazaar to raise money for missions, a thirteenth for mothers of a developmentally disabled child, a fourteenth for young widows, a fifteenth for women who are going through a painful divorce experience, a sixteenth for displaced homemakers who are seeking to enter the labor market, and a seventeenth for younger never-married women who moved to this community for vocational reasons but have neither friends nor kinfolk in this county.

For many, but not all of these women, this circle can be an entry point into a larger role in the life and ministry of the congregation, but first they need the assurance and acceptance offered by this homogeneous circle.

Obviously this plan will be easier to implement if it is part of a larger congregational strategy to (a) increase the degree of diversity within the membership, (b) encourage the existence of homogeneous subgroups in the adult Sunday school, the music program, the recreation program, the men's fellowship, the youth program, and the social life, (c) reinforce the attractiveness of that parish to those who came first to worship there, and (d) affirm redundancy in programming.

While there are many exceptions to this generalization, this concept of intentionally homogeneous subgroups is easier to implement if the worship attendance averages at least 350 on Sunday morning and if the worship attendance-to-members ratio exceeds 70 percent. In other words, a high level of member satisfaction with corporate worship provides a supportive context for this effort by the women's fellowship and other organizations to make this a more inclusive parish.

The Mutual Support Circles

An overlapping, but usually less inclusive approach in terms of nationality, language, and ethnic heritage, is to create three or four or five or six circles for women with a common concern. Again these can be a useful means of expanding the number of entry points. Some of these women subsequently will switch their primary allegiance from that specialized circle to the women's fellowship and/or the congregation as a whole. Most of them, however, enter on the basis that a response is being offered to their needs.

Perhaps the most common is the "New Roots" circle for wives who have moved to this community, not because they wanted to leave where they were, but because their husbands accepted jobs here. (Despite the move toward greater egalitarianism in marriage, in about six out of seven moves, the "trailing spouse" is the wife.)

The husband meets and makes new friends at his place of employment and has a reasonably clearly defined role awaiting his arrival. The wife, who may not have wanted to move, finds her acceptance and meets and makes new friends in the "New Roots" circle of the women's fellowship. This will help her in that difficult process of putting down new roots in what to her is a new community.

This works best, of course, only if (a) the "New Roots" circle exists, (b) it aggressively contacts and invites newcomers, and (c) it is designed to be an inclusionary circle.

A second example is the circle for some of the 670,000 women who have a hysterectomy every year. Despite the widespread feeling this is routine surgery, the subsequent loss of estrogen, the hormonal imbalance, the loss of libido, and the possible second thoughts on the need for this surgery often create concern. Thus the creation of a mutual support group for women who have had a hysterectomy merits consideration. During the past two decades 19 percent of all women age 15 and older have had this surgery. Those 12.6 million women constitute a huge potential audience![4]

A third possibility is a response to a somewhat less common concern. This is the circle designed as a mutual support group for that 8 to 15 percent of all new mothers who find their "post partum blues" evolving into continuing depression. Post-Partum Support International (tel. 215-295-3994 or 805-682-7529) is an umbrella organization designed to offer help in creating mutual support groups.

A fourth possibility is the mutal support group for hurting women. One version of this was mentioned in chapter 2 when Susan Brown and three other friends created a mutual support group for the rejected Jennifer Jefferson. The focus of this ministry may be the women who are the victims of domestic abuse or women who have been discriminated against in their place of employment or have been sexually violated or have been propositioned by a male teacher in a night school class.

A fifth example is the mutual support group for women who have had a mastectomy. A sixth possibility is the C-Section Circle for women who recently had a baby delivered by cesarean procedure. The number of cesarean deliveries in the United States has jumped from 195,000 in 1970 to 934,000 in 1987. Nearly one out of three deliveries for mothers age 35 and over are by cesarean procedure.

A seventh possibility for the special concerns groups are

women who are in an interfaith marriage. An eighth is for women who are half of an interracial marriage. A ninth is for women who are half of an international marriage which also crosses large cultural differences. A tenth could be for women who are experiencing a painful divorce.

At least a few readers may ask, "How can you suggest these mutual support groups should be created under the umbrella of the women's fellowship when earlier such a strong emphasis was placed on making missions the focal point?"

At least four responses can be offered to that question. First, one of the central themes of this book is offering choices. Second, this can be an effective alternative for those women's fellowships seeking to reach new generations of women. Third, for some readers the definition of missions is sufficiently broad to include this form of outreach under that umbrella.

Finally, and of at least equal importance, is the question of who responds to the needs of people in an ever-changing society. For many decades the family, the church, neighbors, lodges, and the school were the primary channels for responding to the needs of people.

In recent years a new response has emerged often identified as "self-help groups." An informed guess is that in 1970 approximately 5 million people in the United States and Canada were members of self-help groups. By 1989 that number had grown to at least 14 or 15 million.

Many see the 800,000-member Alcoholics Anonymous, founded in the mid-1930s by two self-identified drunkards, as the pioneering model.

Today the self-help movement includes a huge variety of groups such as children of Aging Parents, Debtors Anonymous, Women's Association for Research in Menopause (WARM), Gamblers Anonymous, Parents of Near Drowners (POND), GROW (for former mental patients), Cocaine Anonymous, Loners on Wheels, Emphysema Anonymous, Formerly Employed Mothers at Loose Ends (FEMALE), Kleptomaniacs Anonymous, WWL2M (Women Who Love Too Much), Fundamentalists Anonymous, and the American Mall Walkers Club.

At least a few of us are convinced (a) the Christian faith has a message that can make a difference in the lives of people, (b) most congregations are not prepared to organize and nurture self-help or mutual support groups, (c) a substantial majority of the participants in self-help groups are women, and (d) in many congregations the women's fellowship possesses a larger degree of competence in organizational skills than any other component of that congregation. When those four ingredients are mixed together, one product can be the creation of mutual support or self-help circles.

Critics of the self-help movement argue this approach may oversimplify life for some who need professional help and at the same time magnify the importance and power of the problems faced by others. Critics also contend that societal changes, not self-help, is the best approach to many of the problems, such as racism, access to medical care, economic inequality, and sexual coercion. Others question the effectiveness of self-help groups and suggest they often encourage passivity and conformity.

Proponents contend these groups address issues of empowerment, encourage people to take greater control of their own lives, help participants raise their level of self-esteem, enable people to cope more effectively with daily problems, provide emotional support, and encourage participants to develop new skills.

Nearly everyone agrees (a) the number of people participating in self-help or mutual support groups has grown enormously in recent years, and this suggests a need does exist, (b) this movement is a worldwide phenomenon but more widespread in the United States than anywhere else, (c) an increasing number of adults feel free to discuss personal problems openly with other adults, (d) women are far more likely than men to be participants in these groups, (e) the deterioration of the family is one reason behind the growth of this movement and the disappearance of neighborhoods is a second factor, (f) people are increasingly dissatisfied with the impersonality, bureaucratic barriers, and general level of competence of organizations created to respond to human needs (Does that generalization include the churches?), and

(g) more and more people want greater control over their own lives.

From the perspective of the churches the divisive issue may be an either-or question. Should we take the initiative in forming mutual support groups as part of the ministry of our congregation and proclaim the gospel of Jesus Christ as a part of that effort or should we avoid this phenomenon, concentrate our resources on responding to people's spiritual needs, and encourage secular organizations to respond to the needs of those who find help in these groups?

Will the women's fellowship in your congregation take the initiative in responding to this need or should it be the responsibility of some other group or organization in your church? Or should your congregation ignore this whole subject?

The Displaced Homemaker

Overlapping this concept of mutual support or self-help circles is another possibility that merits separate consideration. This is the circle designed to help displaced homemakers find a new beginning in life following the loss of a husband.

The typical member spent fifteen to thirty years as a wife, mother, and homemaker when she was confronted with the loss of the husband who was the sole breadwinner for that family. Sometimes this was by the premature death of her husband, sometimes by divorce, sometimes by separation without a divorce. This homemaker not only finds herself alone, but often she has been left without an adequate income to support herself. She may be convinced she has no marketable skills to sell in the job market and this whole experience has undermined her self-esteem. After being rejected by what appeared to be one or two potential employers, she may be convinced no one wants her.

At this point the women's fellowship intervenes with a circle that affirms her value as a child of God, helps her strengthen her faith as a Christian, encourages her to learn the skills necessary to enter the labor force, helps her deal with her feelings of guilt, raises her level of self-esteem, involves her in a meaningful way in this mutual support group, and assists her in her search for employment.

This can be one of the most redemptive ministries of your church. A significant fringe benefit, but this should be seen as a fringe benefit, not as a goal, is that this can be a significant source of leadership for your women's fellowship.

The Phoenix Circle

Slightly over one-half of the two and one-half million marriages recorded in the United States in 1988 represented the first marriage for both bride and groom. In nearly one-fourth this was the second, or subsequent, marriage for both. For approximately one out of nine this represented the first marriage for the bride, but the groom had been married before. In a slightly fewer number of those weddings the groom had never been married before, but the bride had been married previously.

Another perspective for understanding this pattern of remarriages is the fact that six or seven out of every ten women who have been divorced or widowed will remarry. (The reason for placing divorce before widowhood in that sentence is that ever since 1975 more marriages in the United States have been terminated by divorce than are ended by the death of a spouse.) To be more specific, 89 percent of the wives who were under age 25 when their marriage came to an end will remarry as will 79 percent of those who were 25 to 29 when they lost their spouse, 59 percent of those in their 30s, and 31 percent for those past age 40.[5]

For those congregations (a) willing to broaden the purpose of the women's fellowship, (b) seeking to reach more younger women, and (c) interested in responding to a significant unmet need, this offers the possibility for creating a new circle.

The typical example is the Phoenix Circle (named after the bird in Egyptian mythology that rose renewed from the ashes of the fire that had consumed it to start another new life). This is a circle composed entirely of women who have remarried following divorce or widowhood. In larger congregations this may be a series of circles. One is organized for divorced women in their thirties and forties who have remarried. Later a second circle may be organized for mature widows who have remarried. This may turn into a coed circle. A third circle may be organized for younger women who have remarried and include both widows and those who saw their marriage end in divorce.

Typically these circles are organized around three to five focal points, such as Bible study, sharing, mutual support, meeting and making new friends, intercessory prayer, laughter, raising the level of self-esteem, coming to discuss with an outsider their common agenda, and trips with husbands included.

The New Widows

Most congregations offer a fair-to-good ministry with widowed women. Typically the pastor and a few couples who have been close friends with that couple before the husband's death rally around as a support group. Sometimes this is supplemented by an adult Sunday school class to which this couple had belonged for years.

A radically different approach is to build a mutual support group in that congregation composed entirely of widowed persons and provide them with the training in bereavement patterns, caring, and counseling skills needed for this specialized lay ministry.[6]

A basic premise is the people who are most likely to understand how it feels to be widowed are those who have been through that experience. A second premise is that many of the concepts and skills required to understand and respond to bereavement have been identified and systematized and can be taught. A third is the informal response offered in most congregations following the death of a spouse can be improved by a more intentional and systematic effort. A fourth is there is life after widowhood.

Many of the circles organized around this highly specialized ministry insist this is a ministry *by* widowed persons *to* the recently widowed with the expectation that this will include that recently widowed woman in a long-term relationship with this circle. Others see this as a response to an immediate need as well as an entry point into the larger organization for that widow who previously had not been a member of that women's fellowship. Some of these are coed circles. At least a few expel (this is a friendly, but firm farewell) any widow or widower following marriage.

The Single Issue Social Action Circle

Most Protestant congregations do not have an active social action committee. One means of responding to that need, and also of attracting a new generation of members, is for the women's fellowship to organize a new circle around that theme.

This can become a divisive issue if the agenda is too extensive. Experience suggests the chances of this becoming divisive are reduced and the prospects for making an impact on society are increased if this is organized as a single issue circle rather than as a multi-issue group. This avowed purpose of the group is to influence public (or denominational) policy on a single issue. This is not a direct services organization as described earlier in the Matthew 25:35 circle. The focus might be on public policies affecting youth or pornography or fair housing or drugs or AIDS or hunger or world peace or any one of dozens of causes.

This type of circle in the women's fellowship can become an attractive entry point into the larger organization for women who are not seeking fellowship or study, but are activists seeking allies in a common cause.

Life as a Religious Pilgrimage

Many people perceive the act of uniting with a worshiping community as the final destination in a religious journey. Everyone, including the pastor and the new member, assumes that new member will continue to be a part of that congregation until either a move to another community or death severs that tie.

An increasing number of churchgoers, however, share a different perspective on that religious journey. They see participation in the life of a particular congregation as simply one step on a longer journey. These churchgoers may now be actively involved in the third or fourth different church since they moved into their present residence. They spend a couple of years in one congregation, conclude they have gained all that congregation can offer them in their religious pilgrimage, switch their allegiance to a second church, a few years later they sense an unfulfilled religious need and resume their search by moving on to a third congregation— often crossing denominational lines with each move. This phenomenon is fed by the increasing number of interdenominational and interfaith marriages as well as by that increase in the number of remarriages.

One response could be to expand the role of the women's fellowship to include the care of religious pilgrims and to encourage them to find a home with other like-minded pilgrims in a circle designed for those on a religious pilgrimage. Experience suggests this leads, not to the merger of circles, but to the creation of new groups as these journeys diverge. Instead of accepting the pattern that many of these religious pilgrims tend to move from congregation to congregation, encourage them to seek a new home within your parish.

The Liturgical Dance Group

The past thirty years have brought a renewed interest in religious symbols, liturgy, music, and art as a means of both expressing one's own faith and as a means of sharing the faith with others. The spoken and written word no longer are adequate in communicating the gospel to all the world! As a general pattern, the younger the members, the greater the impatience with a complete reliance on the written and spoken word in worship.

One result is a sharp increase in the number of congregations that include a liturgical dance team who shares in worship several times a year.

If the leaders are willing to expand that umbrella defining the purpose and role of the women's fellowship (and if this has the support of the pastor), this can be an effective means of attracting women born since World War II. (It also may produce a few expressions of disbelief among women born in the first decade or two of this century.)

A need for liturgical dance may not be understood by women born before the Second World War!

—FRIAR TUCK

The Drama Group

Overlapping this but perhaps less controversial and certainly easier to create is the religious drama group. This raises two policy questions. The first is how broad is that umbrella defining purpose. The second concerns the participation of men. Many plays do require male characters.

An outstanding example of a powerful drama that could be used by a women's fellowship interested in offering a powerful witness on hunger and poverty is the musical, *Lazarus*, by Joel Underwood based on Luke 16:19-31. (For information on the availability of *Lazarus* write Bread for the World, 802 Rhode Island Avenue, N.E., Washington, D.C. 20018.)

Travel and Study

One of the most remarkable of all the changes among North Americans that have occurred in the second half of the twentieth century is the increase in the number of people who have visited another continent. Worldwide travel is becoming an accepted part of life for millions of people.

As a result many churches now include either an adult class in the Sunday school or a circle in the women's fellowship that is built around six organizing principles: (1) the thirst for learning, (2) shared experiences, (3) travel, (4) study, (5) fellowship, and (6) welcoming newcomers. Most of these groups need a minimum number in order to qualify for group rates on travel and housing, so they tend to be eager to receive new recruits. Some are intergenerational and include members who long ago celebrated their sixtieth birthday as well as those who recently turned twenty-one.

A typical September-to-June cycle includes a couple of months of study about the places to be visited, the trip, meeting to share reflections about that experience, and planning for next year's trip.

This can become a useful part of the missions education thrust of that women's fellowship. Or the women's fellowship can concentrate on books as the basic resource for studying missions and bemoan the fact the group gradually is growing older and smaller in numbers.

A variation of this travel-study focus has been developed in at least a few congregations in which the women's fellowship (or one circle in the women's organization) builds a relationship with Christian congregations in Japan or Germany or Africa or South America or some other part of the world and exchange visits. One year the church in North America will host a week-long visit from a group from either continent and the following year the reciprocal visit is completed.

Learn a New Skill

A central organizing principle that is widely used in working with groups of teenagers is based on the assumption that everyone enjoys learning a new skill. This has been a key organizing principle in Scouting, in 4-H Clubs, in high school bands, and in dozens of other youth programs. One of the reinforcements in this approach is the chance to "show off" that skill in a parade, at the county fair, or in some other public display.

A parallel is asking a couple of dozen men to take turns preparing and serving breakfast from seven to eight o'clock every Sunday morning as (a) an initial step in organizing a men's fellowship, (b) a means of increasing the size of the crowd for that early worship service, (c) an attractive alternative for the folks who live alone and who come to enjoy a nutritious breakfast and warm fellowship, (d) part

SUNDAY CAN BE THE WOMEN'S DAY OF REST IF THE MEN MAKE BREAKFAST!

Role-reversals are attractive alternatives for Sunday morning growth!
—FRIAR TUCK.

of a larger system to facilitate the assimilation of newcomers into the fellowship of that congregation, (e) one component of a comprehensive strategy to increase male participation, and (f) the "bait" to lure people to join that new adult Sunday school class that meets for about two hours every Sunday morning.

A parallel for the women's fellowship is to organize a sewing (or quilting) circle that (a) includes mature women who enjoy sewing, (b) attracts young women who want to learn to sew (or quilt), (c) produces a useful product (clothes for the children's home or quilts to be sold to raise money for missions), (d) brings women together across generational lines, (e) enables people to learn and perfect new skills, (f) offers an opportunity to "show off" those skills, (g) allows people to express their creativity through their hands, (h) offers enjoyable opportunities for fellowship, (i) provides a safe and non-threatening place to meet and make new friends, (j) creates an atmosphere that enables women to share life experiences with one another, (k) proves to some elderly women who have increasing doubts about their own self-worth that they are valued members of that congregation who can make a useful contribution, and (l) usually has a wide-open door to welcome members since the task often exceeds the number of available hands. ("You know you belong when you know you are needed.")

The Office Volunteers

A variation of that focus on learning and utilizing a new skill is the circle in the women's fellowship organized to provide volunteers to help staff the church office.

A common example is the circle of ten women with two working Monday morning, two Tuesday morning, two Wednesday afternoon, two all day on Thursday, and two on Friday morning.

As a general rule, if local circumstances permit, it is wiser to ask two women to work the same shift rather than, for example, asking one to work mornings and the other to come in for the afternoon. Whenever possible, for reasons of fellowship, mutual accountability, and reinforcing relationships, volunteers always should be asked to work as part of a team, never alone. The task-oriented person who asks one person to work mornings and another to come in for the afternoon is placing an excessive premium on getting the job done and neglecting one of the basic tenets of how to build and nurture a network of volunteers.

Parties for the Developmentally Disabled

Another circle that combines learning a new skill with being part of a team of volunteers and meeting a widely neglected need is the group that plans, schedules, publicizes, and administers parties several times a year for developmentally disabled persons.

Tens of thousands of developmentally disabled children (many in their teens or older) are being reared at home by their parents with other siblings. The developmentally disabled person watches and listens as a brother or sister comes home from a party at someone's home and shares with the parents the exciting time at that event. The developmentally disabled member of that family watches and listens. The unspoken message is, "It's too bad you cannot go to the parties and have fun as I do."

Instead of competing with a sibling who has mastered many more social skills, the developmentally disabled person comes to these parties planned with a level playing field for all. Instead of silently watching a sibling enthusiastically dash off to a friend's birthday party, the developmentally disabled member of that family can talk with Mother about last month's party or ask again about the date for "my next party."

Invitations can be issued through churches that have Sunday school classes for developmentally disabled persons, through the newspaper, and by sending them to individuals. Invitations also should be issued to those living in institutional settings such as a group home. It is wise to ask if teachers or aides can accompany those coming from classes because they know the individuals and their abilities. A generous number of volunteers should be on hand to help with the party, which should be held in a first floor room, if possible, with rest rooms available.

The party may consist of: (a) greeters for the guests as they arrive, helping with coats and name tags, (b) a game to occupy them while everyone arrives, (c) a sing-along (it is difficult to overstate the importance of music), (d) a simple craft to do and take home, (e) occasionally some entertainment, such as a magician, a demonstration of making animal shapes out of balloons, a juggler, an amusing skit, (f) refreshments (this is required, not optional), and (g) simple games until time to leave.

In some communities a transportation committee may be needed to pick up some of the participants and to return them to their place of residence.

In addition to providing a central organizing point for creating a new circle and meeting a genuine need, this also will help sensitize the members to the needs of others, strengthen the community image of that congregation as a caring community, and be consistent with that central purpose of outreach.

Calling in Nursing Homes

Dozens of churches have one circle in the women's fellowship organized to respond to the need to visit lonely residents of nursing homes. Many of these residents not only have outlived their spouses, but also all of their able-bodied friends. Frequently, their children now live hundreds of miles away. For many mature adults a nursing home is not the place to meet and make new friends.

Some of the women in these circles also accept the responsibility for monitoring the quality of care, rectifying areas of neglect, and serving as an advocate for one or more residents.

CAUTION! This may represent the most challenging alternative suggested in this book. It is not always the most pleasant assignment one could seek. This asks the members to accept a difficult servant role which may include only rare words of gratitude from the kinfolk of the person being visited.

Expand the Fellowship

One of the threads running through this book goes back to some of those basic policy questions raised in the opening chapter. What is appropriate for the women's fellowship and what should be the responsibility of the congregation as a whole? When do the leaders of the women's fellowship draw the line and declare, "We don't do that! If that doesn't get done, it doesn't get done. We're not going to try to do everything around here."

Another approach, and one urged repeatedly in this book, is, "If it really is needed and no one else is doing it, maybe the women's fellowship should expend part of their managerial skill in doing that."

One increasingly common example of an unmet need is a result of the fact that the primary point of socialization has moved out of the neighborhood into the place of work. One result is the erosion of the concept of the geographical parish. A second is that in many congregations most members do not know the majority of that congregation.

One response could be for the women's fellowship to organize a series of fellowship events every year (perhaps quarterly?) that include a meal, opportunities for extended conversation in groups of four to seven people, name tags, and a precisely stated and adhered-to time for adjournment. One goal is each participant will depart feeling (a) two acquaintances are now friends, and (b) two or three strangers are now at least acquaintances.

This is largely a managerial and scheduling task. The groups may meet in the homes of members or in the fellowship hall, but the time together should be structured to facilitate the effort by the participants to become better acquainted with one another.

The "ice breaker" for the gathering could be to ask every participant to bring four 3×5 inch slips of white paper on which the participant completes the question, "Who . . . ?" out of that individual's life story. Thus one might bring these four autobiographical questions: "Who was born on a farm in Wisconsin?" "Who met his wife while in fourth grade?" "Who loves cherry pie with ice cream?" "Who cast his first presidential ballot for Thomas Dewey?"

Someone else might bring four slips that read, "Who enjoys playing the piano?" "Who made a hundred dollars a week on her first job?" "Who was born in Rhode Island?" "Who almost drowned in the Atlantic Ocean?"

The point of the questions is not to boast, but to reveal some little known facts about that participant's life that will stimulate conversation, help those present to share experiences, and enable people to know one another better.

After everyone has arrived, the participants sit in a circle, the slips of paper are gathered and shuffled, and the entire deck is passed from person to person. When the deck reaches you, you read the top slip, guess who is identified by that fact, the person to your left guesses next, and so on until everyone has guessed. The person who contributed that question watches passively and may "guess" the name of someone else

to confuse the others. After everyone has guessed, that
person lets the group know the answer. When it turns out a
particular "Who?" question applies to two or three members
of the group, that often reinforces a sense of common
identity and can add to the foundation for a new friendship.

The point is to play games to help people become better
acquainted, not to simply pass the time.

Who Will Come to My Funeral?

"In order to understand what I'm about to tell you,"
explained a forty-eight-year-old woman to her new pastor,
"you need to know I've been married to the same husband for
twenty-five years, and up until eight months ago we had lived
in the same house in Topeka for fourteen years. Five years
ago my father died and my mother continued to live in the
same house in Akron that they had occupied for nearly thirty
years. A couple of years ago it became apparent that my
mother no longer could stay there alone. Finally, she agreed
to move into a small apartment we had found for her a mile
from our house in Topeka. My mother is now seventy-eight
and at her age she does have trouble making new friends, but
she joined our church and I thought she had found a new
group of friends in a circle that is composed largely of people
her age, although several are younger.

"Several months ago," continued this anxious mother of
three, "my husband's employer told him he could choose
between early retirement or a promotion to a much better job
seven hundred miles from where we were. Naturally, my
husband chose the promotion and we left Topeka and came
here. Mother decided she was not up to another move and
chose to stay behind in that apartment. I can understand and
accept that.

"Last night she telephoned me and after a few minutes of
small talk, I asked her how things were going with her circle.
That question unleashed the floodgates! She burst out, 'I
hate the study! I hate those women! I hate the Women's
Fellowship! I hate the meetings! But if I don't go, who will
come to my funeral? What few old friends I left in Akron

won't be able to come all this distance to my funeral!' Now, Pastor, what should I tell my mother when I call her this evening?"

While most younger readers may have difficulty with this as a major goal in life, for many mature adults who have watched their spouse and nearly all their longtime friends die, a pressing question is, "Who will come to my funeral when I die?" This may be an especially difficult issue for those in the late years of life who decided to move far away from the place where the few remaining friends and most of the kinfolk now live.

Before looking at the relevance of this issue to the women's fellowship, it should be pointed out that for centuries a central organizing principle of lodges, veterans' groups, and military organizations has been attendance at the last rites for a deceased comrade. Can this organizing principle, which has carried almost exclusively a "men only" label, be extended to women?

It is true that men are far more likely than women to leave behind a large number of friends and kinfolk among the survivors. That is simply a product of the fact that the life expectancy of the typical fifty-five-year-old female averages five years longer than the life expectancy of the typical fifty-five-year-old male. Women are far more likely than men to outlive their spouse and many of their friends and relatives.

Do you want to encourage the expectation in your women's fellowship that the survivors will make a special effort to attend the memorial service held following the death of a member? Or is that an irrelevant, or possibly diversionary question? The older your members and the older your potential future members, the more reason to place that on the agenda for your next officers' meeting.

Children of Aging Parents

Not completely unrelated to that issue of death is the growing pattern of middle-aged-to-mature adults who live several hundred miles from a surviving parent. As the years pass and that parent's health begins to deteriorate, this can become a fertile source of anxiety, guilt, expense, worry, and frustration.

One response is to form the combination self-help and mutual support circle for women who are facing this concern. It helps to share experiences and this can ease the guilt.

A far more elaborate, complex, and productive response would be to organize a network of circles so a woman in Salina, Kansas, could visit the nearby widowed mother of a daughter who recently moved to Charlotte, North Carolina. This daughter might look after the aging father, who resides in a nursing home in Charlotte, of a woman who now lives in suburban Minneapolis. This Minnesota daughter could check up on the Minneapolis mother of the daughter who has moved to Salina, Kansas.

Building that network would require an entrepreneurial spirit, a computer, an inquisitive mind, a desire to help people expand their opportunities to help others, and a fair degree of patience. It could be initiated by one congregation and encouraged to snowball. It could be organized by the headquarters staff of a denomination and publicized through denominational literature. Or it could be concluded this is not the appropriate responsibility for a Christian women's organization and should be left to professional social workers to do what the churches used to feel called to do.

Adopt a School

An equally valuable, but less complex undertaking for those seeking to focus on unmet needs would be to organize a circle in the women's fellowship around the purpose of becoming a support group for the teacher and one class in a particular elementary school. This could be a central city school in a poverty neighborhood or it could be an isolated rural school with limited resources or it could be a Christian day school affiliated with that denomination. A growing number of congregations now have their own school.

The purpose of this circle is not simply to provide needed

supplies and other incidentals that may be beyond that
teacher's budget, but more important to demonstrate to both
the teacher and the children that someone does care. The
limits of people's imagination represent the boundaries of
what can happen. One possibility, for example, is to provide
clothes for children in need. Another is to help raise the
money necessary for two dozen Black children to spend two
weeks visiting in Africa. Between those points on the spec-
trum hundreds of possibilities exist. One would be to participate in the founding of a new Christian day school.[7]

Teach Parenting Skills

A growing number of experts in the field of early childhood development are convinced the state of our society in
the year 2010 will be influenced greatly by the quality of
parenting of today's children by their mothers and fathers.

Pilot projects and various experimental programs have
demonstrated that (a) parenting skills can be identified, (b)
these skills can be taught and learned, (c) everyone, regardless of social class, education, personality, or family setting
can benefit from help in learning parenting skills, (d) a
remarkably large core of well-organized opposition exists to
any proposal to make family education part of a public school
curriculum, (e) one result of an effective program with
parents is a happier and better adjusted child, (f) a second
result is a happier, less frustrated and more loving and
competent parent, and (g) a third result is society benefits.[8]

Sometimes this will mean the women's fellowship sponsors
events at the church designed to help mothers and fathers
improve their skills as parents. Frequently this will require a
series of visits by the teacher(s) to mothers (often single
parent mothers in public housing) on the parent's turf.

This could be a unilateral effort by a women's fellowship, a
cooperative venture with another congregation that includes
many potential enrollees, and/or a joint venture with a social
services agency.

Perhaps the best approach is when the women's fellowship
sees this as (a) their contribution to a larger congregation-

wide or community-wide family life emphasis, (b) an opportunity to meet future new members of the women's fellowship on the agenda of the participants, not on the agenda of the women's fellowship, and/or (c) a part of an intentional ministry with single parent families.

This has tremendous attraction for those who seek to have a long-term impact on our society and on tomorrow's adults.

Build New Churches

One of the more interesting possibilities in those congregations that (a) place a high priority on outreach, (b) include a substantial number of members in their early retirement years, and (c) accept as part of their responsibility the "planting" or "mothering" of new congregations is the group that is organized to help create new churches. One version is the group that accepts the responsibility to raise the money and purchase the land that will be the meeting place for a new congregation five or ten years hence. A second approach is the group of volunteers who serve as part of the nucleus for a new mission for twelve to twenty-four months. (It should be noted that a majority of these "short term" volunteers usually end up staying with that new mission, rather than returning to their "home church.")

For hundreds of mature adults the most exciting challenge is to spend two or three months every year as part of a crew that constructs the new building or adds a wing to a small and overcrowded meeting place or that builds the parsonage for the mission developer pastor.

This alternative for a new circle in the women's fellowship is more likely to be seen as a live possibility if (a) the regional judicatory of that denomination has an operational church builders program designed to match resources with needs, (b) the congregation does not include enough interested males to offer a men's fellowship, (c) the women's organization is open to inviting men to participate in their new ventures, (d) the officers of the women's organization are eager to investigate new ideas, (e) the pastor is an active supporter of missions in general and new church development in particular, (f) the site for that new building is beyond daily commuting distance (ideally at least several hundred miles distant) so participants must make a firm commitment to this adventure, and (g) both women and men will be welcomed by those in charge at that site.

Several of the big fringe benefits can be traced back to the fact that working together is one of the most effective means of helping people build new friendship ties. One of these fringe benefits is a greater sense of cohesion and unity among those who share in this adventure. A second is this challenge is an excellent means of winning and assimilating new members. A third is the close personal ties that are built with the workers who come from other churches. The fourth is a reinforcement of the denominational ties and of the links to the universal church. A fifth, as has been pointed out earlier, is that many, many adults, both male and female, secure greater satisfaction out of expressing their creativity through manual skills than through verbal skills.

The Number-One Evangelistic Team

Three generalizations apply to the majority of Protestant congregations on the North American continent: (1) they either are on a plateau in size or are shrinking in numbers; (2) they do not have a systematic and continuing effort for enlisting new members; and (3) the members of the women's fellowship are growing older in age and fewer in numbers.

These generalizations are far more likely to apply to churches in those denominations that are shrinking in numbers. A few examples will illustrate this point. Between 1953 and 1988 membership in the Assemblies of God more than quadrupled and the membership in their women's organization also quadrupled. Between the mergers of 1962 and 1986 the baptized membership of the Lutheran Church in America dropped from 3.3 million to 2.9 million, and the membership of the Lutheran Church Women declined in every year but one. Back in 1956 the Women's Society of Christian Service in The Methodist Church reported 1,790,441 mem-

The women's organization is often a church's number-one evangelistic team!

—FRIAR TUCK

bers, and the counterpart in the Evangelical United Brethren Church reported 180,000 members. In 1986 the successor denomination, The United Methodist Church, reported a total of 1,165,879 members in the United Methodist Women. (It also should be noted that in 1956 the women in the two predecessor denominations raised or contributed a combined total of $29 million—equivalent, after allowing for inflation, to $115 million in 1986 buying power. In 1986 the total raised by local units was $55 million. Or if one thinks in terms of current dollars, per capita personal income in the United States rose from $1,965 in 1956 to $14,140 in 1986.) The reported membership of The General Conference Mennonite Church dropped by approximately 2 percent between 1965 and 1987, but the membership of Women in Mission rose by nearly 30 percent. The Evangelical Covenant Church reported an increase in membership of nearly one-fourth between 1973 and 1988 and the number of women in Covenant Women increased by one-third during those same years.

The point of that long paragraph is membership in the women's organization is more likely to drop if the combined membership of all churches is shrinking and more likely to increase if that denomination is experiencing a large influx of new members.

Therefore, it should not be seen as an unreasonable goal for a women's fellowship interested in reaching a new generation of younger members to make that a high priority for that congregation (or denomination).

Thus the "project" for next year for your women's fellowship could be to invite several hundred people to your church. One round of invitations could go out to invite people to worship with you in one of your Christmas Eve services next December 24. An earlier round could invite children to the Vacation Bible School this summer. A third round could be sent to mothers inviting them to share in your newly created Mothers' Morning Out program

IT'S TOUGH BEING HERE, TOUGHER STILL TO BE IGNORED WHILE I AM HERE!

A varied approach can rescue those who fall through the cracks of general programming! —FRIAR TUCK

every Tuesday. Another set of invitations could invite people to come worship with you at a special Labor Day Sunday morning service in which you plan to recognize all the educators in your community. The possibilities are endless.

The two basic requirements are (1) something to which nonmembers could be invited and if they came, they would not feel like outsiders, but rather like welcomed guests (that usually means the combination Homecoming-Anniversary celebration does not qualify) or better yet, like pioneers invited in to help plan and implement something new, and (2) a redundant and persistent system for inviting people.

The big risk is what if you try it and it works? What if you invite people and they come?

At the top of that list of consequences is the need to make these nonmembers feel welcome and glad they came. You want them to leave pleased with what happened and looking forward to a possible return visit. You need to build a list of the names and addresses of those who came so they can be invited back. You need to be planning the next event or program to which nonmembers will be invited.

What if the vast majority of those who come are women? Are you prepared to expand the women's fellowship to include new circles or groups for these newcomers? Or will you expect them to be welcomed into long-established groups? What will this do to your congregation if women now constitute 60 percent or more of those present for Sunday morning worship? Will that proportion rise to 70 percent?

What if your efforts result in a doubling of the membership? Will the old-timers welcome these newcomers? Will you have to expand the Sunday morning schedule to accommodate people with two worship experiences? Will your pastor be supportive of the changes that will be required? Will some of the long-tenured leaders feel threatened? Will they protest, "The tail is wagging the dog"? Will those who are convinced the women's fellowship should concentrate on missions, not evangelism, feel this is a subversion of purpose? Will you be able to incorporate the newcomers as leaders and officers in this congregation? Or would it be easier and more comfortable to grow older together and watch the numbers diminish?

Go Coed

During the past few decades several women's colleges have opened their doors to welcome male students. Every year the number of male nurses and the number of male secretaries continues to climb. Scores of what once were all-male business, professional, and social clubs have begun to admit women. Historically all-male occupations and vocations have been opened to accept women. Likewise organizations and vocations that formerly were limited to women are now accepting men. Every year the number of fathers who remain at home to care for the children while the mother leaves for work has increased. Gender lines do not represent the barriers they once did. Likewise what once were all-Black institutions of higher education, such as Lincoln University in Missouri, Kentucky State University, and a dozen similar schools now enroll large numbers of white students. Younger adults no longer are willing to fit comfortably into the compartments created by earlier generations.

One possibility for the women's fellowship in your church could be to open the door to men. In several congregations the first step in this direction was to accept the contributions of men to the annual bazaar. In others this is now clearly a coed enterprise and men are both wanted and needed because of the increase in the size of the bazaar. (One version is to take the bazaar out of the basement or fellowship hall, place it under a tent in the lot next to the building, turn it into an auction, expand the number of peripheral events, schedule it for Homecoming weekend, and triple the net proceeds. That requires a lot of help!)

In other congregations the women's fellowship has created a new coed circle to provide a warm welcome for younger childless couples who are separated all day at work and want to be together in whatever discretionary time they have left.

In dozens of churches the women's fellowship has undertaken a new ministry or is offering a new program directed at couples. Examples include the travel and study circle, the church builders club, the teaching of parenting skills, caring for aging parents, the drama group, the advocacy circle, the single issue social action circle, the adopt-a-school circle, and the charismatic renewal circle.

Perhaps the outstanding example of going coed was accomplished by the Church of the Nazarene in 1952, but a brief bit of history is necessary to understand the context.

Back in April 1899 "a few sisters met and organized a society to be known as the Woman's Missionary Society with eight charter members." By 1907 this had grown to eighteen auxiliaries with a membership of approximately 400. It was not until 1915, however, that the Society was officially recognized as an auxiliary organization of the Church of the Nazarene. It was understood the primary role of the Society would be to support that denomination's Board of Foreign Missions. In 1928 the name was changed to the Women's Foreign Missionary Society, and the focus was clearly world missions including enlisting missionaries, prayer, missionary education, raising money, and challenging young people with the possibilities of a call to the mission field. When the denomination's Department of World Missions was confronted with a severe financial crisis in 1949, the women helped meet and resolve that crisis.

This part of the organization's history, which once was nicknamed the "Dustpan Brigade," has its parallels in several denominations. The distinctive part of this story, however, came in 1952 and was symbolized by dropping any reference to women in the name of the organization and changing it to the Nazarene World Missionary Society. That was part of the decision to include men as active and full-fledged members. It may not be a coincidence that the membership has climbed from 125,891 in 1956 to 552,769 in 1988.

One of the reasons for that growth in membership has been the opening of the door wider to include women, men, youth, and children. More important, however, has been (a) the clarity of purpose and vision, (b) the focus on the Great Commission (Matt. 28:18-20) and missions, (c) the denominational commitment to world missions, (d) the commitment and competence of the leaders, (e) the remarkably strong support from the Board of General Superintendents, and (f) the "Work and Witness" program that challenges both women and men to give of themselves in mission work-camp experiences all around the world. A focus on missions can overcome differences of gender.

Should this be on the list of possibilities for your church?

Raise Expectations!

The long-term pattern in several denominations, in thousands of congregations, and in many women's fellowships has been to lower the requirements of those who want to become members. Two of the most common products of those efforts to include more people by lowering the requirements for membership have been (1) an increase in the proportion of members with a relatively low level of participation and (2) a decrease in the number of active members.

For two thousand years the Christian faith has challenged people with what many concluded were excessively high expectations. Examples range from abstinence from what was defined as unacceptable behavior to tithing to regular attendance at worship to vows of poverty.

Today literally thousands of Protestant congregations on the North American continent report that their attendance at the major weekly worship service greatly exceeds their membership. Many expect members to return to the Lord the tithe that is His and to contribute 5 percent or 7 percent or 10 percent of their income over and above that tithe.

As you seek to revitalize the women's fellowship in your church, one alternative is to seek to include more women by reducing expectations, by cutting back from twelve to four general meetings annually, and by not requiring regular attendance.

A more productive route may be to become more optimistic about the level of people's commitment to raise the level of expectations, to invite potential future members to help give birth to the new rather than concentrating resources on keeping dying traditions alive for another year or two, and by challenging people to exceed their self-imposed limitations.

What do you think?

Notes

Chapter One

1. For a more extensive discussion of this distinction between a movement and an organization see Kenneth I. Winston, ed., *The Principles of Social Order* (Durham, N.C.: Duke University Press, 1981), or Lyle E. Schaller, *Getting Things Done* (Nashville: Abingdon Press, 1986), chapter 2.
2. A discussion of the differences between small groups and large groups can be found in Lyle E. Schaller, *Effective Church Planning* (Nashville: Abingdon Press, 1979), pp. 17-63. See chapter 4 of this book for a brief introduction to large group dynamics.
3. See Lyle E. Schaller, "How Large Is Your Choir?" *Choristers Guild Letters*, January 1985, pp. 83-85.
4. Richard A. Gabriel and Paul L. Savage, *Crisis in Command* (New York: Hill & Wang, 1978).
5. See Lyle E. Schaller, *Reflections of a Contrarian* (Nashville: Abingdon Press, 1989), chapter 4.
6. For a more comprehensive discussion of endowment funds see Lyle E. Schaller and Edward Lee Tucker, *44 Ways to Expand the Financial Base of Your Congregation* (Nashville: Abingdon Press, 1989), chapter 5.
7. Barry Sussman, *What Americans Really Think* (New York: Pantheon Books, 1988), p. 206.
8. Lyle E. Schaller, *It's a Different World!* (Nashville: Abingdon Press, 1987), p. 11.
9. Viviana A. Zelizer, *Pricing the Priceless Child* (New York: Basic Books, 1985), pp. 113-37.
10. Theodore Levitt, *Innovation in Marketing* (New York: McGraw-Hill, 1962).
11. See Brad Edmondson, "Bringing in the Sheaves," *American Demographics*, August 1988, pp. 28-32.

Chapter Two

1. Nancy Gibbs, "High Noon for Women's Clubs," *Time*, May 30, 1988.

2. *Statistical Abstract of the United States 1988* (Washington, D.C.: Bureau of the Census, 1988). See also Earl F. Mellor and William Parks II, "A Year's Work: labor force activity from a different perspective," *Monthly Labor Review*, September 1988, pp. 13-18.

3. A discussion of alternative career tracks for mothers who want to practice law can be found in Jennifer A. Kingston, "Women in the Law Say Path Is Limited by 'Mommy Track,' " *New York Times*, Monday, August 8, 1988, and David Margolisk, "At the Bar," *New York Times*, November 11, 1988. For two provocative articles on the "Mommy Track," see Felice N. Schwartz, "Management Women and the New Facts of Life," *Harvard Business Review*, January-February 1989, pp. 65-76 and Anne Keller, "The Mommy Track," *Business Week*, March 20, 1989, pp. 126-34. For her response to the many critics, also see Felice N. Schwartz, "The 'Mommy Track' Isn't Anti-Woman," *New York Times*, March 22, 1989.

4. For a discussion of this point see Michael Barone, "The Presidency: Mama's Boys and Papa's Prides," *Washington Post National Weekly Edition*, August 8-14, 1988.

Chapter Five

1. An excellent periodical, if the goal is to alleviate world hunger, is *Seeds*, 222 East Lake Drive, Decatur, Georgia 30030. Another potential ally is Bread for the World, 802 Rhode Island Avenue, N.E., Washington, D.C. 20018.

2. For an introduction to this concept see William H. Thompson, "A Nursing Home Project," *Bird Watcher's Digest*, May/June 1988, pp. 68-73. The preliminary research suggests this can be a useful means of improving the life satisfaction, alertness, sociability, happiness, and sense of decision-making power of nursing home residents.

3. See Herbert Mitgang, "Libraries in Crisis Over Cost of Journals," *New York Times*, September 5, 1988.

4. Vickie Hufnagel, *No More Hysterectomies* (New York: NAL Penguin, 1988).

5. These estimates are the work of Larry Bumpass, a professor at the University of Wisconsin in Madison, James Sweet, and Teresa Castro and were presented in a paper delivered at the 1988 annual meeting of the American Sociological Association in Atlanta.

6. Scores of books have been published in recent years on widowhood and bereavement. Among the most useful are Ira O. Glick, et al., *The First Year of Bereavement* (New York: John Wiley & Sons, 1974); Helena Z. Lopata, *Widowhood in an*

American City (Cambridge, Ma.: Schenkman Publishing Co., 1972); Lynn Caine, *Widow* (New York: William Morrow & Co., 1974); Alfred Allan Lewis and Barrie Berns, *Three Out of Four Wives* (New York: Macmillan Publishing Co., 1975); Andrew J. Cherlin, *Marriage, Divorce, Remarriage* (Cambridge, Ma: Harvard University Press, 1981); Charlotte Foehner and Carol Cozart, *Widow's Handbook: A Guide for Living* (Golden, Colo.: Fulcrum, 1987).

7. For a brief discussion of the changing clientele of private Christian schools see Lyle E. Schaller, *It's a Different World!* (Nashville: Abingdon Press, 1987), pp. 103-11.

8. For a brief, but exceptionally well-organized introduction to the teaching of parenting skills see Bettye M. Caldwell, "Education of Families for Parenting," in Michael W. Yogman and T. Berry Brazelton, eds., *In Support of Families* (Cambridge, Ma.: Harvard University Press, 1986). A provocative analysis of the implications of three decades of changes in the role of women in American society can be found in Victor R. Fuchs, *Women's Quest for Economic Equality* (Cambridge, Ma.: Harvard University Press, 1988).